STEVE S

ISIS DAWN

SPECIAL FORCES WAR IN SYRIA & IRAQ

CW00866164

© Steve Stone 2015

Steve Stone has asserted his rights under the Copyright, Design and Patents Act, 1988, to be identified as the author of this work.

Published by Digital Dream Publishing 2015

ISBN-13: 978-1517188863

ISBN-10: 1517188865

CONTENTS

AUTHOR'S NOTE

Whilst this book has been thoroughly researched, any inaccuracies are down to the author. With a vast array of information, a small amount of which is conflicting, as with anything based around war and politics, a true and accurate 'bigger picture' can be hard to fully come by. This book tries to not only describe the sort of mission our brave military forces are undertaking, but ISIS, both in terms of its history and current tactics, along with a small element of middle east history to put everything in context. Any errors found will be corrected in future editions, as this story is still evolving and the book essentially a snapshot of current operations.

One clear element is the bravery of all the Special Forces, intelligence and support services involved in the war against ISIS – SAS, Delta, SEAL Team Six, SBS and other international forces involved. They are risking their lives to bring peace and stability to a foreign land - to stop the spread of another even more vicious terrorist organisation across the globe. One that is even more extreme than al-Qaeda.

FOREWORD

In May 2015, a joint operation between the SAS and Delta Force was undertaken to take out Abu Sayyaf a top ISIS financier. The SAS was tasked with performing reconnaissance on the target before Delta operators being directed by the SAS went in to take out Sayyaf. This would see yet another ferocious battle being fought by heroic Special Forces. The SAS went in wearing American uniforms and carrying American weapons to keep their participation secret. The SAS troopers were flown into Deir ez-Zor governorate, Syria by a V-22 Osprey a tilt rotor aircraft designed for vertical takeoff and landing (VTOL), and short takeoff and landing (STOL) capability. It combines the functionality of a conventional helicopter with the long-range, high-speed cruise performance of a turboprop aircraft.

They moved from their LZ and onto their reconnaissance area close to the compound that Sayyaf was staying at. They dug themselves into a heavily camouflaged position. Over a period of several days the SAS had eyes on the target with telescopic cameras and night vision goggles. They observed all movements in and out as well as the location of all personnel within the compound. The SAS were soon able to confirm Sayyaf's presence and provide a detailed picture for Delta to use to mount a raid to kill or capture Sayyaf.

Initially F-18 Hornets strafed the ISIS compound just before the arrival of 50 Delta operators keen to get stuck into their mission. The MH-60 Pave Hawks once they had inserted the Delta Operators began to give cover for them with an onslaught of rockets and 7.62 mm miniguns. This did not fully quell the resistance and Delta still had to fight through at times in hand to hand battle with ISIS fighters before finally being overwhelmed.

With the compound secure Delta Operators could search the building for any intelligence, especially any relating to ISIS money making schemes. The SAS also joined in by putting a cutoff all the way round the compound to prevent any ISIS fighters escaping alive. During the raid a total of fifteen ISIS fighters were killed including Sayyaf who succumbed to Delta's firepower. Sayyaf's wife was also captured and a Yazidi slave girl was rescued. In the official release the SAS did not get a mention as per their wishes to ensure that potential political issues of British boots on the ground in Syria. It was sources close to the Kurdish government who disclosed details of the SAS's role.

On 21st October 2015 a raid was launched just east of the ISIS stronghold of Hawija, in northern Iraq, in the largely Kurdish region of Kirkuk. The raid targeted a prison run by ISIS militants in the mostly Kurdish province of Kirkuk. The raid was to rescue 70 being held hostage by ISIS in Iraq as the prisoners were due to be executed. The compound being used as a prison had bar concrete walls and floor with rubble strewn everywhere. After the intense firefight bullet holes could be seem on most of the walls, although some may have been from earlier battles in and around the compound. The ensuing firefight Delta found themselves in was without a doubt very intense. This was room to room fighting taking out ISIS fighters as they went.

During the raid six ISIS fighters were killed along with a further 20 wounded. American airstrikes were used to destroy roads leading to the site, to prevent ISIS fighters from making an escape.

Four Peshmerga soldiers from the organised local Kurdish Militia were wounded during the fierce firefight that ensued. This raid also sadly, saw the loss of the first American soldier in operations against ISIS. A Delta operator, Master Sergeant Joshua Wheeler was shot and later died of his injuries, bringing home the real danger Special Forces face mounting a war against fanatics. These missions are typical of many that are covered in more detail in this book along with the background on the 'Rise of ISIS' to give you a real insight into the harsh and bloody war against fanatics.

INTRODUCTION

ISIS has become synonymous with brutal killings, slavery and the barbaric use of women as sex slaves. There is no doubt that they have managed to elevate themselves to the most horrific terrorist army the world has ever known. In some respects, we are in a third world war as ISIS has planned and in some cases managed to carry out attacks across the world and will continue to attempt do so as this new war unfolds – with no quick solution.

Many attacks have been foiled by US, British and European intelligence and law agencies. ISIS has conducted one of the best online recruitment campaigns and have been able to indoctrinate many simply through social media. Many of these have been isolated or disaffected young people who yearn for excitement. One of ISIS's more elaborate videos based on a game state, "This is your call of duty." Such videos are extremely impacting on young people helping to recruit them into what they perceive as the righteous and glamourous ISIS.

The term "lone wolf" or 'lone actor' has been used increasingly with individual extremist's intent on trying to undertake attacks across the western world, in particular America and the UK. One example being 24 year old Mohammad Youssuf Abdulazeez who on July 16, 2015 shot four U.S. Marines dead and one U.S. Navy sailor who died in hospital two days later, in two separate recruiting offices in Chattanooga, Tennessee. He was described as "quiet and friendly" and with an interest in wrestling and mixed martial arts, Abulazeez had, in recent months, turned more toward Islam, growing a beard and attending weekly religious services. Before carrying out his atrocities and loosing is own life in the process. However, he showed no signs prior to the shootings of becoming an extremist. But he still went on to unleash a barrage of bullets from an AK-47-style weapon, before being shot by Police Officers after confronting him.

These indoctrinated individuals are of a greater threat as they almost decide one day, they will carry out an atrocity. They often remain hidden in communities, their families unaware of their intentions or radicalisation. Other than a change in their thoughts towards their religion. Although it is unfair to even slightly allow ISIS to be shown as religious - they are terrorists, no religion actually states it is right to kill. Some may say the right for retribution under certain strict circumstances however.

This is where the background intelligence gathered by the FBI, MI5, Special Branch and local police forces. Even from community leaders is so vital in stopping a war that is not simply based in Iraq and Syria. One high profile example, Mohammed Emwazi was also known in the media as Jihadi John, knew British security services were closing in on him and that he was a "dead man walking" following some revealing emails sent to a British Journalist. The emails were sent before he left Britain to join ISIS in Syria - during a time when MI5 suspected him of being a terrorist, however, Mohammed saw himself as the victim and on the verge of suicide due to the intrusion. Mohammed believed himself to be a victim - went on orchestrate at least six hostage murders in Syria after joining ISIS. At the time of being followed by MI5, Mohammed was a member of a secret Osama Bin Laden sleeper cell based in Britain called 'The London Boys', which planned to carry out atrocities in the West. He was involved with a violent street gang who targeted the wealthy residents of Belgravia, Central London with stun guns. 'Jihadi John was finally neutralized by a drone attack as he stepped into his car on November 12, 2015.

The sad tragedy at Charlie Hebdo magazine in Paris in which 12 innocents were brutally murdered followed by the even more devastating attack on November 13, 2015 by radical extremists. Shows the extremes this new wave of extremists will go to. They now threaten not only world security, but freedom of speech and freedom of expression. Whilst we all need to be sensitive to one another, tolerance is also important. In no way should life be taken in the manner they have in Paris and elsewhere. We are in many ways at a turning point and the next few months and years will see sadly not only more attacks, but policy and law changes to equip the world to battle this threat to world security. The battle this time is not only in defined areas, but our own towns and cities and in the cyber world. Cybercrime is seeing an exponential rise and this includes malicious attacks or hacking where messages of defiance or DOS (Denial Of Service) attacks are on the rise as a way to bring fear and a show of force or control. The Hacktivists 'Anonymous' have announced their intentions to attack and hack extremists after the attacks in Paris, bringing a whole new dimension to the war against ISIS. This book focuses on Iraq and Syria and the impact of the SAS and Delta Force there. Although the SBS and SEALs are all doing their bit to chop off the head of a snake and turn the tide on ISIS as well. U.S Special Forces have fought some of their bloodiest battles since Vietnam on the streets of Ramadi and Fallujah in Iraq. The war against ISIS in the larger scheme of things is now global with global security forces on a high state of alert. The

British Royal Air Force, has alone spent some £37 million over 126 bombing missions in 2014 alone using Tornado GR4 bombers to kill around 195 ISIS fighters. Deploying Paveway bombs along with Brimstone missiles and finally Hellfire missiles fired from Predator drones. Although this has made some progress the war against ISIS is a hard one, they are tenacious fighters and have managed to gather up a wide range of arms and recruit thousands from across the globe into their ranks. The Iraqi Army is struggling and foreign boots on the ground after Iraq and Afghanistan is currently a political and world hot potato. Although, special forces and other specialist forces are on the ground helping to support the war with covert missions, target designation and training of opposing forces. But, there is no quick solution - the world and all faiths must unite to get rid of extremism from its local communities and stem the flow of radicalisation.

Jonathan Gilliam an ex US Navy SEAL, FBI Special Agent and Federal Air Marshal in a recent interview, gave 6 poignant points about ISIS and the strategy to combat them in a recent interview.3. What separates ISIS from other terrorist groups.

After the beheading of James Foley, his killer said, you are no longer fighting an insurgency, you are fighting an Islamic State. Remember, you have 30,000 people claiming to be part of the Islamic State. Groups like al-Qaeda could never measure up, they might have had 30,000 fighters, but they were spread all over the place. Here's what separates ISIS from other groups: they have the numbers, they have the dollars, they have the technology – and they have the will.

4. It's not just about the numbers.

The more people ISIS recruits, the more powerful it will be. It's not the number of people ISIS has, it's the ferocity with which they fight.

5. ISIS threat to the American homeland.

As far as ISIS and their ability to attack here, there's no telling what they could bring across the border with the kind of money they have at their disposal. If they wanted to, they could purchase an entire arsenal.

6. How ISIS sympathizers should be treated.

And these Americans who go fight for ISIS don't deserve to be given the same treatment as someone who commits a crime in the United States. They are burning their passports, that's really like saying you don't want to be a citizen anymore. If they return to the U.S., they should be treated as war criminals. If you fight for the enemy, you should lose your citizenship."

CHAPTER ONE – SCUD

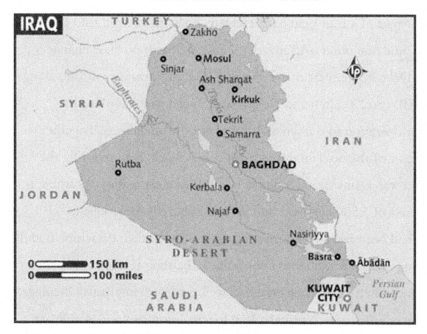

Northern Iraq 17:00 hrs August 2014

The arrow like form of two American F-18 Super Hornets roared over our heads, on its way to bomb another ISIS position. Looking from our rocky outcrop the Iraqi desert stretched out in front of us with Tal Afar to our east. We were half way between Sinjar and Tal Afar. ISIS took Tel Afar on June 23, 2014, which included the airport. ISIS then advanced on and took Sinjar on August 3, 2014, which was the prelude to the authorisation of US bombing missions on the August 7. After they had killed 500 Yazidis who are a Kurdish ethno-religious community whose syncretic but ancient religion is Yazidism. The Yazidis had escaped to Mount Sinjar, a craggy, mile-high ridge identified in local legend as the final resting place of Noah's ark. Mount Sinjar was where an estimated 40,000 Iraqi people had become trapped

13

and lacked food and water, after ISIS had threatened genocide to anyone who would not convert to Islam.

I was part of a four man patrol which consisted of Sgt Deko an old sweat, and one other SAS trooper, King and Scott on an exchange from Delta Force. Part of a wider SAS and SRS presence in Iraq along with SBS, Seal Team 6 and Delta Force. Delta were involved in a similar operation to ours in a different area of operations. Together we were part of the now infamous Task Force Black. Set up during the second war against Iraq designed as a hunter killer team responsible for the arrest of 3,500 terrorists and several hundreds more killed.

We had been tasked with meeting up with a Kurdish detachment and offering them our skills and knowledge in battling ISIS or as it wants to now be known IS (Islamic State), as well as identifying British jihadists. We have been out in Northern Iraq for two months now, initially we had been tasked with reconnaissance patrols, locating ISIS positions and gathering intelligence on their size and location. Iraq covers an area of 169,234 sq miles compared to 94,060 sq miles for the UK. Iraq only has a small coastal area with Turkey, Syria, Jordan and Saudia Arabia on one side and Iran on the other, with Kuwait at the bottom. Initially our operations were kept to Northern Iraq, concentrating on halting the progress of ISIS and starting to dismantle industrial scale insurgency, just as we have done in Afghanistan. ISIS is thought to have around 50,000 fighters in Syria and 30,000 in Iraq.

They have swept through Iraq with ease and taken control of towns and oil wells. ISIS follow a similar pattern when they take control of a town. They quickly secure the water, flour and energy (oil and gas) resources of the area, centralising distribution and thereby making the local population dependent on ISIS for survival. ISIS exports about 9,000 barrels of oil per day from Iraq - with prices ranging from about £15-£27 ($25-$45). Some of this oil goes to Kurdish middlemen up towards Turkey, some of the oil goes for domestic ISIS consumption and some goes to the Assad regime, which in turn sells weapons back to the group. It is a classic war economy as IS needs munitions on top of the ones it has seized. For this, ISIS needs money to purchase them. Money is also needed for the widespread propaganda and recruitment campaign. ISIS fighters need to be fed and watered and this also costs money. ISIS is believed, to have assets of around$2bn up from $900m after ISIS captured Mosul in June 2014. ISIS is thought to have taken hundreds of millions of dollars from Mosul's branch of Iraq's central bank. One of the biggest factors, along with the oil in ISIS taking over Iraq was the need for more powerful weapons to aid in the war in Syria. ISIS has suffered several defeats in Syria and needed to not only grow in size, but have the weapons to take on both the government forces and rebel forces that were trying to get rid of ISIS from Syria.

Today, we were off on another recce mission, looking for further military positions for a bombing mission. We moved off at twilight using the cover of darkness to hide our movements. Being August it was very hot during the day around 40 degrees and at night dropped to a bit more comfortable 27 degrees. We were not too far from Mosul, which had been taken over by IS after they swept in on June 10, 2014. The local people have been living in a state of fear and limbo – fear of the brutality of ISIS, and in limbo, not knowing when or if, the Iraqi government or international forces will push them out. Half a million

15

people escaped on foot or by car in the first 48 hours, but more than a million of them remain.

Our area of operation is quite vast and currently, in the main, we are undertaking recce patrols between Sinjar and Mosul, picking out enemy positions and vectoring in airstrike's on IS positions. A couple of hours into our patrol we could see a strange silhouette in the distance. It looked very much like some form of military position. We could see patrols around the position, but needed to get in closer to identify the position before we could decide the best course of action. I am not a fan of recce patrols, I suppose I always want a taste of action, but currently the Regiment is involved in intelligence gathering and support more than anything else, at various hot spots round the world. Afghanistan was very hands on with an element of intelligence gathering. If you go back to the dark days of Northern Ireland and the fight against the IRA. It was intelligence as opposed to killing that led to a peace process. As information is power and all the intelligence gathered was then used in negotiations to begin about the armistice and the peace process. Although, this is a very simplistic analogy of the secret war against IRA. Which was long before my time in the Regiment.

ISIS like al-Qaeda will not negotiate, it is their way or the highway, pardoning the pun. The only way to get rid of these fanatics is to drop them, better with a 7.62 than a 5.56 round with their greater stopping power. Our patrol objective was not to engage as their numbers were vastly superior to the four of us and we were still very much trying to operate in secret even though there have already been numerous media leaks, some intentional as part of a wider physiological war with ISIS.

We went down on our belt buckles and made use of any available cover as we slowly moved towards the enemy position. It was a dark moonless night, but the sky was clear and you could see the stars shining brightly in the sky. The ground we crawled over was hard and dusty with short but spiky grass. We continued to move up onto the ISIS position, stopping, motionless, to allow a small patrol to pass, before continuing to a suitable point. The military position we had come across was a SCUD launcher complete with a SCUD missile. The Regiment had come up against these in the first Iraq War and the now famous Bravo Two Zero raid. The SCUD is essentially a ballistic missile carried on the back on the back of an 8 wheeled truck. It was developed during the height of the cold war and in use by numerous countries around the world. Even America, have four that were converted into targets by Lockheed Martin. This missile and its launcher needed to be destroyed before it could be deployed or drive off to a new position. We made a note of its position and moved back a safe distance to send a report back to GCHQ, to arrange an airstrike. GCHQ is a security and intelligence organisation tasked by the British Government to protect Britain from threats.

Getting a message through proved more difficult than expected. Due to the volume of air traffic and reduced availability, it took some time to get a response. Regiment HQ pushed through though for an air strike, as a high priority target. As twilight approached, we moved into better cover waiting the imminent attack. We knew ISIS potentially had Scuds, but Iraq is so vast and even with all our various eyes in the sky on both the UK and US side. With Predator drones, our Sentinel R1 and RC-135, US E3 Senty and American RC-135, backed up with satellites, intelligence gathering is very high tech business these days.

It was not long before the high-pitched roar of a jet's exhaust filled our ears. Two A-10C Thunderbolts broke into view on the horizon coming in, a few hundred feet. They looked so ungainly in the air, with their blunt nose and twin engines high up at the rear, yet packed a formidable punch. The A-10s streaked towards us contour flying on a low-level ground attack mission. The A-10s began wheeling and swooping like hungry Eagles searching for prey. The first jet went into a dive, before dropping a 500lb bomb. The large black object plummeted earthwards and buried itself into the ground next to a vehicle. The force of the blast blew the entire vehicle into the air, engulfing it in a thick cloud of smoke and blasted sand. As the air cleared, I could see saw the launcher sitting where it had landed - it had been thrown almost at right-angles to its original position. The second A10, amidst a barrage of machine gun fire, let rip with a hail of 30 mm rounds from its Avenger cannon. After each pass they pulled up violently, twisting and dodging, stretched to the limits of their capabilities, to escape away from the small arms fire. More bullets, and then the second A-10 dropped another 500lb bomb. The smoke-filled air was then filled again with another blinding flash and a thunderous explosion. The pair of A-10s had made short work of the SCUD and its launcher, which was now totally obliterated as black smoke poured out, of what was left of the burnt, mangled and twisted mass that use to be a Scud launcher.

Several ISIS fighters lay dead around the launcher as the smell of cordite hung in the air. Up until September 2, 2014 the US have undertaken 143 airstrikes, 90 of these have been on the Mosul Dam the largest dam in Iraq, captured by the ISIS from the Kurds along with Mosul and Tel Afar. The Kurdish fighters call themselves Peshmerga, which means "those who confront death." The Peshmerga forces of Kurdistan have existed since the advent of the Kurdish independence movement in the early 1920s, following the collapse of the Ottoman and Qajar empires which had jointly ruled over the area. The Kurdish army has been formed out of the Peshmerga. They are usually armed with AKMs (Modernised AK-47 rifles), RPKs (lightweight 7.62 machine gun) and DShKs (heavy infantry machine gun). During the American-led invasion of Iraq in 2003, the Peshmerga captured the rest of the arms of the Iraqi forces, consisting of more than 2,000 armoured vehicles and a number of artillery pieces. From August 2014, they have been receiving arms from western countries to aid in the fight against ISIS.

Mosul dam was captured by the ISIS on August 7, 2014. The ISIS control of the dam created fears that its power supply could be interrupted or even hold the local populous to ransom over energy. Another worry was the potential for ISIS to breach the dam and cause widespread flooding. With US airstrikes destroying 19 vehicles belonging to IS, as well as a checkpoint near the dam. ISIS were only able to hold onto the dam for 10 days when on August 17, 2014, Peshmerga and the Iraqi Army launched a successful operation to retake control of the dam from ISIS militants. By August 18, the Peshmerga and Iraqi military had regained complete control of the dam. Below are all the airstrikes and their positions carried out by the US up to September 7, 2014.

Once the A-10s had finished their business, we made good our escape to find a better position to lay up for the day and get some well-earned rest before moving off. My mouth and throat felt as though I'd been chewing hot ashes. As soon as we stopped, I got a brew on quick time to feel a little bit more refreshed, even though we were resting; one of us had to be on guard duty. I had four hours until my stint, so got a bit of shut eye after a brew and some scoff. I quickly drifted off into a deep sleep, snoring loudly apparently.

Sgt Deko was 5'11" with a thin build and receding ginger air, he had eight years in the Regiment, double my four after passing selection. He was originally from Sittingbourne in Kent and initially joined the Para's, where he did six years leaving as a corporal to pass selection and be demoted back to a trooper. Although once you have gained your Special Forces skills, you gain your Special Forces pay which would be more than Deko was on as a corporal. Deko intended doing two more years, as he would be close to forty and a good age to retire from the Regiment. Like many he intended to get himself on the 'circuit' picking up work using the skills gained from the Regiment. King was the baby of the group having only just passed selection under a year ago, at 22 he had plenty to learn. He had already been on several ops around the world, learning things much quicker than I had. Originally from Wales he was a Signaller or Scaley as we called them, prior to going through selection. He was a bugger for playing jokes on people. His jokes had come close to getting him kicked out the regiment twice, as they tended to be aimed at officers who he completely disliked and distrusted. In the field, though, you could rely on him 100% to have your back and keep you safe. He was fearless in battle and in many ways just the sort

20

of guy you wanted with you, when fighting fanatics like ISIS who also showed no fear. Finally, there was Scott, at 6'4 with a broad Texan accent - we nicknamed him 'Dallas' partly as he was actually from Dallas and partly as he looked like Bobby Uwing out of the 80s TV series Dallas. He had a small amount of fame from his high school years as an American football player. We all took the piss though, as why do they need to wear all those pads? They don't in English Rugby. Banter aside, Dallas was a brilliant soldier and ex U.S. Army Ranger with an ability to sense the enemy before any of us had seen them!

With our mission changing from not only recce, but also supporting Kurdish soldiers and the hunting down of key members and the so called Jihadist John. This would mean us, making face to face contact with extremists, who could be totally unpredictable. We had tech on our side with drones and a biometric reader to ascertain exactly who we were dealing with. All information is relayed from our position via a portable satellite manned by a Scaly from 264 (SAS) Signal Squadron, who sends it to a spy plane, such as a RC-135 aircraft, circling overhead.

Inside the RC-135, a 17-man team processes the information and send it back to GCHQ. At GCHQ all information it is analysed. The information on British Jihadists is matched against records of British jihadi believed to be fighting in Syria and Iraq, before 'feedback information' is sent back to us.

GCHQ's library is said to include recordings of thousands of voices taken from phone and radio intercepts. Meanwhile, on the Turkish-Syrian border, SRR soldiers fly drones into IS strongholds and give live details of their movements.

The SRR's drones can fly for up to 24 hours, climbing to an altitude of more than 18,000ft. From here they are able to survey hundreds of miles of territory occupied by ISIS fighters, and gather valuable intelligence on ISIS positions and size of the forces involved, they however are still not a full replacement for good old MK1 eyes on the target. The Regiment knows Iraq well after having fought in two wars and this has proved invaluable, with maps, terrain and climate. Understanding the locals and how best to interact and gain support from the local populace, is something else that the Regiment learnt from the last war in Iraq. Along with intelligence and directing airstrikes on ISIS positions, we also have to help train and support the various military forces. Although, the Iraqi national army has proven ineffective, even after tens of billions have been spent on its equipment and training. The Kurdish Pershmerga has lost some of its famed fighting spirit and cannot be relied upon to fight in the interests of a coalition outside of its own territory. Iraqi's Shia militia, are being thrown into the fight - and some have proven as venal as ISIS - murdering Sunnis and torching their homes. Sunni militia are the key and need to be turned against ISIS - but how far their loyalties would lie once they have secured their own local security is impossible to say. Local, national and international politics have a large part to play in the final outcome.

CHAPTER TWO - THE RISE OF ISIS

Religious wars have raged for thousands of years from the Christian Crusades to al-Quaeda and ISIS today. Religion has often been used as a way to justify a war or reasons to start a war. Often these religious views have been skewed or altered to justify killing. ISIS (Islamic State of Iraq and Siryia) is a Sunni jihadist group. Not to be confused with Isis, which is a goddess from Ancient Egyptian religious beliefs. Whose worship spread throughout the Greco-Roman world. ISIS has become synonymous with its vicious behaviour following beheadings, crucifixions, stoning's, massacres, burying victims alive and religious and ethnic cleansing. ISIS adheres to a doctrine of war without any limits or constraints. They do not believe in arbitration or compromise when it comes to settling disputes.

ISIS emerged from radical Sunni jihadists in Iraq who fought under the banner "al-Qaeda in Iraq." Their goal since being founded in 2004 has been to create a hard line Islamic state crossing over the borders of Syria and Iraq. The single most important factor in ISIS's recent resurgence is the conflict between Iraqi Shias and Iraqi Sunnis. The majority of Iraqis – between 60% and 70% - are Shias. However ex-dictator Saddam Hussein was a Sunni and the absolute power of his Ba'ath party gave Sunnis the belief that they are the real majority and legitimate rulers. The difference between the two largest Muslim groups originated with a controversy over who got to take power after the Prophet Muhammad's death in 632AD. Abu Bakr was chosen as caliph, but a minority of Muslims favoured another man, Ali. Ali's followers became known as Shiat Ali, partisans of Ali – Shias. In 656,

Ali became the fourth caliph after Abu Bakr was assassinated. Some Muslims, the ancestors of today's Sunnis, rebelled against him. Ali himself was assassinated in 661 after violence spread.

ISIS has also been called ISIL (Islamic State of Iraq and the Levant). Then on June 29, 2014, ISIS announced the establishment of a new caliphate - meaning succession, and the group formally changed its name to the Islamic State (IS). ISIS have self-proclaimed status for religious authority over all Muslims across the world. They wish to bring Muslim inhabited regions around the world under its political control. Starting with Iraq, Syria and territory in the Levant region, which includes Jordan, Israel, Palestine, Lebanon, Cyprus and an area in southern Turkey that includes Hatay. Lead by Abu Bakr al-Baghdadi, who is believed to have been born in Samarra, north of Baghdad, in 1971 and joined the insurgency that erupted in Iraq soon after the 2003 US led invasion. al-Baghdadi was in custody at a US detention facility in Iraq until 2009 when he was handed over to the Iraqi authorities. As he left Camp Bucca, near Iraq's southern border with Kuwait, he told his captors: "I'll see you guys in New York." It has been claimed that al-Baghdadi, who uses a variety of aliases, was only radicalised while in US custody. According to this story, he was a farmer wrongly swept up and became a follower of bin Laden at Camp Bucca. However, it is more likely al-Baghdadi was an Islamic fundamentalist before the US and Britain invaded Iraq. In 2010 he emerged as the leader of al-Qaeda in Iraq, one of the groups that later became IS. In 2012, sensing an opportunity, al-Baghdadi dispatched some foot soldiers to join the fighting against Bashar al-Assad's government in Syria. In 2013 he announced that the group was merging with Jabhat al-Nusra, the other al-Qaida affiliate in Syria, to form a new group called the Islamic State in Iraq and al-Sham. Nusra, predominantly Syrian in membership, is more focused on the overthrow of Assad, whereas ISIS is more international and interested in expanding its territory and enforcing Shariah law.

The pull of ISIS for many, is that it has outperformed all other similar organisations in combat and put in place a slick media campaign, using social media in dozens of languages to attract young men and women to its cause, something that ISIS has been very successful at. Money has initially poured in from countries and individuals keen to see Assad removed from power, but unaware of the true nature of ISIS until more recently. ISIS has been very successful and recruiting young people from around the world.

ISIS is light years ahead in every activity - from fighting, to organisation and hierarchy, to media messaging. One example is a feature-length film released online called Swords IV, which includes a slow-motion bomb sequence reminiscent of The Hurt Locker, aerial footage that nods to Zero Dark Thirty, and scenes filmed through the crosshairs of a sniper rifle that wouldn't look out of place in a first-person shoot-'em-up. Another example of the shrewd use of social media, is when ISIS attacked Mosul in Iraq in June, analysts stated that their propaganda made the fighting easier. In wars gone by, advancing armies smoothed their path with missiles. IS instead did this with tweets and a movie. Thousands of their Twitter followers installed an app – called the Dawn of Glad Tidings. This app allows ISIS to use their accounts to send out centrally written updates. Released simultaneously, the messages swamp social media, giving ISIS a far larger online reach than their own accounts would otherwise allow. The Dawn app pumps out news of ISIS advances, gory images, or frightening videos like Swords IV – creating the impression of an uncontrollable and unstoppable force. This propaganda worked in Mosul - Iraqi soldiers fled their posts (thirty-thousand Iraqi troops ran from 800 IS fighters), thinking they would face a gruesome fate if they were captured in uniform. Something they were not prepared to do along with sectarianism also playing a role and the reason the Iraq military, although, superior in numbers and weapons has been ineffective against ISIS.

ISIS have become known as a terrorist organisation in the western world due to war crimes and atrocities they have already committed. There is no doubt that they are a security threat and an organisation that is still growing and attracting members (Jihdists) from around the world. ISIS can be thought of as a successor to Al Qaeda in Iraq. Under its leader, Abu Bakr al-Baghdadi, ISIS has grown significantly, gaining support in Iraq due to alleged economic and political discrimination against Arab Iraqi Sunnis, and establishing a large presence in the Syrian governorates of Ar-Raqqah, Idlib, Deir ez-Zor and Aleppo after entering the Syrian Civil War. Abu Bakr al-Baghdadi has ensured he has appointed a rigid chain of command under is hardline leadership. He has divided command into separate councils responsible for everything from the sale of oil, to internal communications and decisions on which prisoners to execute and how.

What these terrorist organisations have used is the word 'Jihadist,' and used their interpretation as a reason to undertake a 'holy war' particularly western civilisation that they see as the root of all evil.

The SAS was initially on the ground to monitor the IS threat in both Iraq and Syria, but became part of an operation to rescue an estimated 40,000 "desperate" Iraqi refugees, exposed, starving and dying of thirst" in temperatures of 50C. This initial rescue operation has then become widened to take out key ISIS leaders, support Iraqi and other forces against ISIS and search or the 'Jihadist John' the generic name given to British citizens that have joined ISIS and undertaken war crimes.

Initially, the SAS had been deployed to northern Iraq to gather intelligence ahead of any potential rescue operation, led by the US, to airlift thousands of Yazidi refugees from Mount Sinjar. SAS soldiers initially moved to the region near Mount Sinjar where US Special Forces were coordinating the rescue effort, to gather ISIS positions and get a much needed battle picture before any rescue mission could begin. The intelligence involved the size of forces and their current military equipment, some of which had been seized by the ISIS as they overran defending Iraqi forces. Although the number of refugees found on Mount Sinjar was found to be less than had initially been predicted. The UK also announced that it would send Soviet-era ammunition from eastern European countries to Kurdish forces fighting ISIS in northern Iraq. The EU has grave concerns about how swiftly ISIS forces are spreading across Iraq and Syria and the German foreign ministry warned of, "an existential threat to ethnic and religious minorities in Iraq, for the state and for the whole region." ISIS is a clear and present danger and with ever increasing numbers joining from inside western countries propose a real terrorist threat along the lines of both 9/11 and 7/7. These Jihadist's want to be killed as dying to them leads to martyrdom as they believe they are carrying out religious duties and cleansing the world of infidels and those that go against their religious beliefs.

What is the worst part of all of this is that it could all be avoided with a bit of tolerance and understanding. I lack any form of tolerance and have very blinkered views. Everyone has a right to be who they want to be and believe what they want to believe, through freedom of choice. No religion or belief is more important than another, they are all important with different religious paths. In an ideal world, people should be free to choose their path and indeed choose not to follow any belief or religion.

CHAPTER THREE – DAM IT

Near Mosul Dam 0300 hrs

In the first few moments of the attack, we decamped our vehicles to get our eyes on where the attack was coming from. It was from our five o'clock position - we could hear the unmistakable noise of the 12.7mm rounds fleeing from a DShK and impacting around us. Some rounds ricocheting back into the air, these rounds would tear through, both our body armour and Toyota 4x4s. It was not hard to work out where the rounds were coming from though - we just had to follow the tracer rounds back to where they were spewing out from, creating bright orange flashes against the inky black sky.

Deko and the rest of the troop knew all too soon that more weapons would open up. ISIS was unlikely to have opened up with only one DShK. We were all scanning the terrain to the southeast of our position, convinced that this was just the start of whatever the ISIS had in store for us. Not long after the DShK had opened up several other sources of tracer began to fly over our heads. We had located the DShK, but now had small arms fire to locate and get some brass down on them.

I swung my weapon around to engage the numerous targets, seeing if I could spot a body to fire at. I could feel the rounds whooshing inches above my head, the rest of the lads were also hunting down individual targets and starting to get some rounds off, in the direction of the incoming fire. Deko started shouting "GET SOME FUCKING FIRE AT THAT FUCKING DSHK!" The lads knew what they needed to do before Deko had opened his mouth; we needed to knock that

DSHK out before it took us out. We were pinned down, and may have been able to jump into our 4x4s, hit the gas and escape into the night. But it it was standard operating procedure when you were ambushed in a good defensive position to stay put and fight it out. The issue ere was, that we were not really in a good defensive position.

Deko instructed two of us to outflank them and get on the rear of the position. Meanwhile, King was on the 7.62 GPMG (General Purpose Machine Gun) and getting some serious suppressing fire down on the position that had opened up on us. The ISIS had a commanding position elevated with a slight lip. They were still partially hidden from view, but still adjusting their arc of fire to become more effective. Our wagons had yet to take any rounds, amazingly, but it would only be a matter of time. We estimated that there was probably one truck with a DShK mounted on it and two or three fighters with AKs. We were not sure if they had clocked us driving past, or had been following us, wondering what three Toyota pickups were doing in the middle of the desert in the early hours. We had been heading towards Mosul Dam to to get eyes on it and gather intel on ISIS positions. Somehow, we had stumbled across a local patrol and were now fully engaged with it.

I could just make out the form of the enemy gunner, and that meant I could target him. I indicated towards the position as Smart and Rai, began to make their way round to the right flank of the enemy position. I could easily see the distinctive flash of a muzzle, and in the glare of the weapon firing I could see the unmistakable silhouette of a DShK. I let off several controlled shots at the silhouette that was firing the gun. I could sense my rounds were falling a fraction short. They were sparking wildly, as they rebounded off the ridge lying between me and the DShK. I raised myself on the balls of my feet and brought the barrel up a fraction, and fired again. I saw my rounds spark and flare as they tore into the metal of the IS truck.

The ISIS fighter on the DShK had swung round slightly and revealed himself to us; we pounded him with the GPMG as well. Meanwhile, Smart and Rai had made it round to the side of the Truck with the DShK mounted on it. They decided to move up closer and chuck a grenade in. With very little cover they moved up to the position slowly, one of our rounds had hit the ISIS fighter on the DShK in the shoulder, as we saw his body shudder from the impact, however, he just kept on blatting away, keeping his finger hard on the trigger, unleashing a long and savage burst in our direction.

Rai removed the pin to the grenade and lobbed it in – the grenade landed right in the back of the truck, the ISIS fighter on the DShK, had not noticed the grenade land. He had total tunnel vision, as he focused on us. A few seconds passed, BOOM! A bright orange flash lit up the desert and a hot flame shot into the sky. The smoke and dust settled, the DShK now lay silent. We took this as our cue to get moving and jumped into the Toyota's as Smart and Rai came storming back before jumping into the cab of one of the Toyota's. We hit the gas as the truck wheels scrabbled slightly, trying to get a grip in the soft sandy ground. The truck wheels kicking up a cloud of dust, that would of helped hide us from the small arms fire we could still hear, as we made good our escape into the night. You cannot deny the focused and tenacious fighting spirit of IS. Their fighting prowess is second to none, they are well trained and disciplined, in many ways the complete opposite to the Iraqi Army.

Although, ISIS did have close links with al-Qaeda until February 2014 when al-Qaeda cut ties with the group following an eight month power struggle. They cited that brutality and "notorious intractability" for cutting ties to ISIS. Their ultimate aim is to ensure strict Sharia law and ensure that only those that follow the Muslim way of life are allowed to live. Those that refuse to convert have been killed in Iraq, leading to condemnation by countries around the world and leading to military aid, initially with air strikes. However, as in Syria, Special Forces have been on the ground gathering intelligence before going out to capture Jihadists. In particular those from the US and the UK, thought to be involved in war crimes. It is thought as many as 500 UK citizens have gone to fight with ISIS in Iraq and Syria. They have been recruited through indoctrination and the promise of excitement and being a "true Muslim." ISIS's sophisticated outreach campaign appeals to disaffected and deluded young Sunnis worldwide because it is seen as a powerful vanguard that delivers victory and salvation. Far from regarding ISIS with disgust in regard to ISIS's brutality, young recruits are attracted by its shock-and-awe tactics against the enemies of Islam. They are impressed by its military prowess and impressive campaign. Each victory brings more recruits to ISIS. Nothing succeeds like success, and ISIS military gains have brought it a recruitment bonanza. Its exploits on the battlefield - especially capturing huge swathes of territory in Syria and Iraq, and establishing a caliphate have brought the group accolade from disaffected western Muslims, wanting to be part of a tight-knit community with a very strong identity.

UK authorities have withdrawn 23 passports this year and made 69 arrests in a bid to stop the flow of fighters travelling to Iraq and Syria.

These terrorists must not be confused with the majority of Muslims who have publicly denounced both al-Quaeda and ISIS.

Chapter Four – Night Attack

Northern Iraq 00:00 hrs

A week later, after being ambushed, we were off to recce a larger ISIS position in preparation for an attack. At around midnight, we found our target. We were about three quarters of a mile away as we sat and observed the ISIS fighters. We then began to circle the position to get a better view gathering intelligence in preparation for an attack. As soon as it was first light, it was time to lay low and go into hiding for the day. That night, another patrol moved off, but the ground made it hard going for the vehicles.

After two and a half hours of driving, they had still not yet reached our position. The final part of the journey involved crossing an Iraqi motorway. The area was a hive of activity, with various ISIS patrols going up and down, most likely looking for military units or Iraq security forces. The problem with crossing the motorway was that the bridge was unsafe and the motorway had a large drainage ditch running down the side of it, which was too deep for our vehicles to cross.

They had no choice but to travel a further few miles down a deserted motorway with no lights on, looking for a suitable position to cross. They found a junction and left the motorway. Once across motorway they were not that far from Mosul and our position attacking an enemy base just outside Mosul. There was a lot of activity at the site and a constant stream of ISIS fighters entering and leaving the area. We continued to gather intelligence and pass it on for a raid the following night.

We were to go in and take down as many fighters as possible as well as destroying their communications, although much of ISIS communications is undertaken using mobile phones. If we could seize an ISIS commander's phone, we could then integrate it forensically. This would most likely yield phone numbers for various IS fighters and other useful numbers that would subsequently be used to aid with tracking them down. With the all the necessary intelligence, and after several messages to the Head Shed, a raid on the ISIS base was planned. Sentries guarded the main gate to the ISIS base. The plan was to drive within a mile of the objective and use the vehicles as fire support. A recce group would then go forward, along with close fire support. The recce team would then guide the rest of the SAS troopers onto the target, which was to clear the building, destroy equipment along with the seizure of a mobile phone or phones along with any other useful intelligence. During the initial attack, an anti-tank missile would be fired – one missile at the sentry position sent in by Kurdish soldiers. Explosives would then be placed on the perimeter fence, with the three assault teams affecting entry on the buildings. The building complex had a main building a several smaller buildings all two storeys. Inside the main building, the floors were connected by a stairway near the building entrance and one assault team was assigned to each floor.

Once the ISIS fighters had been slotted, it would be time to try and gather as much intelligence as possible before ISIS reinforcements arrived. There was no doubt in my mind it would be a difficult mission, attacking fanatics that would keep coming at you until quite literally you had shot life out of them. It was for this reason we switched from our usual 5.56 C8 to a Hekler & Koch HK417Special Forces 7.62

weapon, which is essentially an HK416 chambered for 7.62×51mm ammunition for greater stopping power, whilst still getting plenty of brass down. British Amy doctrine has always been to injure, so other soldiers then have to come and take away their wounded. In Afghanistan this tactic has not worked, as the wounded get left and often are so high on Opium keep coming for you until they drop dead.

The patrol commander, Captain Fox outlined where the fire support would be positioned and where the assault would start. As soon as that was complete, it was time to prepare for the attack. The final part of the briefing involved the groupings; we were all told, which team they would be on. RHQ had an enormous amount of intelligence on the building, but very little of the enemies' strength. Two troops in total would undertake the attack.

The afternoon was spent preparing for the assault, making sure essential equipment was packed and working. At 6:30pm the convoy of vehicles moved out as the darkness swept over and the temperature started to drop. We were only a mile from our objective and we held short to make sure there were no ISIS patrols about before moving into our first RV with some Peshmerga who were going to give us some fire support. As we got close to the objective, a couple of man-made trenches dug in long lines meant the vehicles had to detour slightly before finally coming to their forward position about half a mile from our FUP (Forming Up Point).

After doing a final recce on the objective, it became clear that IS had quite a few vehicles, that looked like Toyota Hilux's, some with weapons, possibly a DSHKs and .50 cal mounted on them along with other ISIS fighters milling about some carrying RPDs. We decided to dismount and move up to the objective on foot for a frontal assault. The Peshmerga would be on our right flank, offering fire support. We were in luck tonight with cloud cover making the night time sky dark enough to cover our movement. We made the assumption that the IS would not think to use night vision goggles, even if they possessed any. Their tactics and the way they fought was almost identical to the Taliban having attended the same training camps and some IS fighters, being veterans of the Afghan and Iraq wars.

It was not long before we hit the main entrance road and began to move down it, staying low. Further along, we moved behind a small escarpment that ran alongside the road. We were now in the middle of a large enemy position, trying to formulate a new plan. With a new plan of action, we all moved off, and lay up behind a large sand bank about 200 yards from our objective.

The base was surrounded by a wall, behind which there could be a second perimeter fence. A lead scout was sent in to give an early warning to the rest of the team. As the lead scout moved forward, more detail of the objective came into view. As we moved up towards a road, we held short and went into all-round defence. We would need to cross a road and move over open ground to make it to the objective. Before the scout headed back to the rest of the SAS team to report their findings. With this further information on the target it was decided to utilise some of the team to give flank protection, while the main group, consisting of the demolition teams and close fire support, moved up towards the main base building.

The team pushed forward, before noticing a pile of sandbags in a corner that looked like an enemy position. This position was empty, so we continued forward another few hundred feet. We were very nearly spotted by an open truck carrying a group of ISIS fighters all brandishing an AK-47 and a couple had RPG-7 RPGs (Rocket Propelled Grenades). An RPG is designed to fragment into hundreds of shards of razor-sharp steel, which are blasted forward from the point of the explosion, fanning out and tearing flesh or light armour to shreds. RPG rounds can be set to either airburst mode going off after a set distance midair or explode on impact in detonating mode. The Taliban has used airburst mode to bring down helicopters by setting the RPGs to explode close enough for the shrapnel to shred hydraulic lines and electrical wiring looms.

We managed to dive behind a battered and battle damaged BMP just in time. Nearby, a truck complete would serve as a good observation position. It was funny to see an American Humvee driving around complete with a US M240B machine gun mounted on top. Even though, the M240B was deadly, firing around 750 -950 7.62 rounds a minute and a 1,800m effective range. The demolition team started their move towards their assigned objectives as the Peshmerga fire support team got into position. There was an almost eerie silence that made everything seem a bit too calm. The darkness seemed to have enveloped everything and my mind became focused on the mission, blocking out everything else. The silence was interrupted by a mumbling coming from inside the cab of the truck. The cab contained a young IS fighter of about fourteen or fifteen years. He was soon awoken by the two SAS soldiers, who had no choice, but to bind and gag him, normally it would have been a double tap to the head, but he was felt to be too young to kill. If he had shown any resistance or tried to point his unloaded AK47 at us, then we may have had no choice. Once bound and gagged, we rolled him under the truck, in between the four rear wheels. Unfortunately, we had been spotted by an IS fighter and almost instantaneously, small arms fire opened up followed by a 12.7mm DSHK. These Russian anti-aircraft guns could churn out 600 rounds per minute. It made a highly effective ground attack weapon that could shred lightly armoured vehicles, tearing through walls and even trees. The odd tracer rounds were now whizzing across the sky, bringing some limited light to the gloom, before ricocheting or impacting the ground. The fire was completely random and it was obvious the IS had no idea where we were, or even who we were. However, we were now compromised and there was little point remaining stealthy. We gave the order to the Peshmerga to start laying down covering fire as we moved up onto the main objective. The Peshmerga fired an RPG at exactly the right point to knock the main gate out, dispensing of the guards at the same time.

Small arms fire was now coming from all directions as we drew closer. It was still wildly inaccurate, but it must not be forgotten that the AK47 is only really accurate to about 50 metres, it is much better at putting a lot of brass down with good short range stopping power. We moved up onto the main building one team took the upper floor ad one team took the lower floor in classic, SAS room by room clearance and a double tap to the head, followed by a couple of shots into the body once they were on the ground to ensure they were dead. We were ever vigil for any signs of booby traps using our experience and knowledge of IEDs and their placements from the Regiments time in Afghanistan. Any useful intelligence material was gathered up before

39

we got out as quickly as we could, knowing reinforcements would be on their way.

ISIS fighters had already begun to regroup from our surprise attack and the effective fire support from the Peshmerga. We now had no choice but to run the gauntlet, back to our FUP (Forming Up Point). We ran like mad to find cover, and luckily not one of us was hit, here was allot of brass coming down, but it was still ineffective and flying in all directions. After we had cleared the perimeter the enemy fire seemed to become more intense, but was only partially effective. The team quickly got into formation and began our retreat from the area. As we drew close to the FUP, two ISIS fighters opened up on us, hitting one of the teams through the sleeve on his shoulder. This added a little bit of confusion and caused the team to split up, looking for better cover. One of the lads managed to get a couple of rounds into a DShK gunner. The rounds hit the gunner side on, pushing him slightly side wards before he slumped forward over the DShK, and for an instant it fell silent. But a split second later a second fighter had climbed onto the weapon, and the DShK's gaping muzzle began spitting fire in our direction once more.

It was going to be a slow fighting retreat as thousands of rounds buzzed all round us as more IS fighters seem to pop up, almost as if they had been buried in the ground and we were in the midst of some form of zombie apocalypse. The Peshmerga continued to offer fire support, but our own fire support needed to pull back as well, with us giving them covering fire, as they made a hasty retreat back to the FUP. We did slot a few fighters as we made our fighting retreat. Before we got into our vehicles and shot off, back into the desert and the cover of darkness. The op was considered a success and we had gathered up highly useful intelligence that would be useful for planning and coordination of further attacks. It would also aid us in the training of the Peshmerga and Iraqi military, giving them valuable insight and intelligence. Any IS defeats was a blow to their propaganda machine. We needed to prove to the local forces, especially the Iraqi military that IS was not invincible and no match for highly trained professional soldiers.

Chapter Five - Iraq

The first Gulf war was caused by the Iraqi invasion of Kuwait. The Gulf War started on August 2, 1990. It was caused by the heavy debts incurred by Iraq and the conflict centred around Iraq's claims that Kuwait was Iraqi territory. After the ceasefire with Iran was signed in August 1988, Iraq was heavily debt-ridden. Most of its debt was owed to Saudi Arabia and Kuwait. Iraq pressured both nations to forgive the debts, but they refused. This lead to Saddam Hussain's decision to invade Kuwait. The operation to remove Saddam Hussein and his army from Kuwait was called 'Operation Desert Storm' and lasted from January 17 to February 28, 1991.

During the first Gulf War, some hundred thousand Iraqi soldiers died. Many were killed by the intense bombing that took place during the war. The SAS was initially tasked with reconnaissance and lazering targets for allied aircraft to bomb. This was followed by hunting for Scud missiles and destroying them. In the second Gulf War the SAS was employed once again to aid in the capture of key players including Saddam Hussein. They worked alongside the SBS, Seal Team 6 and Delta Force as part of Task Force Black.

The second war in Iraq consisted of two phases. The first was an invasion of Iraq, which started on March 20, 2003. It was led by a US invasion force and ultimately led to the end of Ba'athist Iraq and removal of Saddam Hussein from power. Following the initial invasion phase a second longer phase of fighting, in which an insurgency emerged to oppose the occupying forces and the newly formed Iraqi government. Around 96 percent of the casualties suffered by the U.S.

led coalition were suffered during the second phase, rather than the initial invasion. The United States fully withdrew from Iraq in December 2011, although Special Forces have still been present, with links to Al-Quaeda and more recently IS.

A Central Intelligence Agency invasion team entered Iraq on July 10, 2002. This CIA team was composed of members of the CIA's Special Activities Division and was later joined by members of the US military's elite Joint Special Operations Command (JSOC). Together, they prepared for the invasion of conventional forces. These efforts consisted of persuading the commanders of several Iraqi military divisions to surrender rather than oppose the invasion, and to identify all of the initial leadership targets during very high risk reconnaissance missions. The idea was to ensure as little resistance as possible to reduce casualties, especially on the coalition side. The most important element was to get the Kurdish Peshmerga organised, so they could become the Northern front of the invasion. They were able to defeat Ansar al-Islam in Iraqi Kurdistan before the invasion and then went on to defeat the Iraqi Army in the north. During these defeats, a large number of militants were killed and a chemical weapons facility was found at Sargat.

At 5:34 am Baghdad time on March 20, 2003 the military invasion of Iraq began. The invasion was led by led by US Army General Tommy Franks, initially being called Operation Iraqi Liberation, but was later renamed to Operation Iraqi Freedom, the UK and the Australian coalition forces cooperated with Kurdish Peshmerga forces in the north. Approximately forty other governments participated in the operation by providing troops, equipment, services, security, and special forces, with 248,000 soldiers from the United States, 45,000 British soldiers, 2,000 Australian soldiers and 194, Polish soldiers from Special Forces unit GROM sent to Kuwait for the invasion. The invasion force was also supported by Iraqi Kurdish militia troops, estimated to number upwards of 70,000. The objectives of the invasion, was to end the regime of Saddam Hussein. Then, to identify, isolate and eliminate Iraq's weapons of mass destruction. Search for, to capture and to drive out terrorists from Iraq. Collect such intelligence related to terrorist networks. Collect intelligence related to the global network of illicit weapons of mass destruction. Be able to end sanctions and to immediately deliver humanitarian support to the displaced and too many needy Iraqi citizens. Secure Iraq's oil fields and resources, which belonged to the Iraqi people. Finally, to help the Iraqi people create conditions for a transition to a representative self-government. The invasion was very quick even though heavy mounts of resistance were encountered. The Iraqi regime still had a large force with armoured divisions to fight the coalition forces with. Coalition troops launched an air and amphibious assault on the Al-Faw peninsula to secure the oil fields and the important ports, supported by warships of the Royal Navy, Polish Navy, and Royal Australian Navy. The United States Marine Corps' 15th Marine Expeditionary Unit, attached to 3 Commando Brigade and the Polish Special Forces unit GROM attacked the port of Umm Qasr, while the British Army's 16 Air Assault Brigade secured the oil fields in southern Iraq. The heavy armour of the US 3rd Infantry Division moved westward and then northward through the western desert toward Baghdad, while the 1st Marine Expeditionary Force moved more easterly along Highway 1 through the centre of the country, and 1 British Armoured Division moved northward through the eastern marshland. The US 1st Marine Division fought through Nasiriyah in a battle to seize the major road junction and nearby Talil Airfield. The United States Army 3rd Infantry Division defeated Iraqi forces entrenched in and around the airfield.

With the Nasiriyah and Talil Airfields secured to its rear, the 3rd Infantry Division supported by 101st Airborne Division continued to attack north toward Najaf and Karbala, but a severe sand storm slowed the coalition advance and there was a halt to consolidate and make sure the supply lines were secure. When they started again, they secured the Karbala Gap, a key approach to Baghdad. The bridges over the Euphrates River were secured, and the American forces moved through the gap towards Baghdad. In the middle of Iraq, the 1st Marine Division fought its way to the eastern side of Baghdad, and prepared for the attack on Baghdad to seize it.

Bagdad fell on April 9, 2003 ending Saddam Hussein's rule that had lasted 24 years. The Ba'ath Party was removed from power. The Iraqi people felt free, however, this left a power vacuum, and room for terrorist parties to start to pop up and wreak havoc. In many ways, Iraq has become more unstable after the removal of the hard-line dictatorship and is still struggling to maintain security. With the Iraqi military defeated the secret war in Iraq and Task Force Black sprang into action, not only to capture and search for Saddam Hussein and his commanders, but to help quell the terrorist uprising as best as they could. This inability to control and get rid of various terrorist organisations US troops and allied Sunni militias defeated al-Qaeda in Iraq during the post-2006 troop surge, however the surge did not destroy its fighters completely. This left Iraq ripe for IS to move in and try to take over the country by force. The SAS had a hard time in Iraq, as did all the armed and Special Forces. On September 19, 2005, two SAS soldiers were on a surveillance operation in an unmarked car, close to the Jamiyat police station in Basra, Iraq. The SAS had been tasked with investigating claims that the Iraqi police had been torturing prisoners in the station. One particular senior police officer was suspected, and it was he who the two-man SAS team were watching.

The surveillance team was heading back when their army-supplied car broke down and they had no choice but to get a taxi out of the area. When they reached an army checkpoint, which was believed to be a set-up, they were marched into an outhouse next door, stripped naked, blindfolded and handcuffed before being bundled into a car and taken to a police station. At the station, they were thrown into a cell and tortured with mock executions; a pistol barrel was placed into the backs of their heads and the captors pretended to fire, even though the gun was not loaded. This was one of many mock executions the SAS hostages would endure, carried out by what was thought to be the local militia during the nine hours they were held hostage. One of the prisoners, Colin Maclachlan, had already received a head wound during the arrest. MacLauchlan had been involved in Operation Barras to rescue hostages in Sierra Leon in 2001 and had directly taken part in the rescue mission.

Outside the police station could be heard shouting from rioters, along with gunfire and explosions. A British army, police officer wandered into the station and on hearing his British accent, Maclachlan shouted out that they were SAS soldiers being held hostage. The Iraqi police

46

tried to convince the British officer that they were actually Egyptian terrorists, but the officer was not convinced and went to get help. Troops were sent in, in the form of two warrior tanks. However, the tanks came under attack from petrol bombs, and the crew from one of the tanks, Sgt George Long of the Staffordshire Regiment, had his uniform partially set alight by a petrol bomb. He had no choice but to leap from the tank and roll on the ground to put the flames out. These images were captured by news teams and spread by the media across the world. With the increasingly hostile crowd, the warrior tanks had no choice but to make a tactical withdrawal. The local militia had armed the angry mob with petrol bombs to use against the British forces. The British Embassy had already used its official channels to request the release of the two SAS men. The Iraq interior ministry issued an order for their release, but this was duly ignored. A team of SAS were sitting in the back of a C130 some 130 miles away waiting for the order to go, as the commanders fought to get the green light. The SAS knew the security forces in Jamiat were preparing to withstand an attack. They had men being brought in with rocket-propelled grenades. In the end, the SAS Lieutenant Colonel gave the order to go and was told that he could only mount a rescue mission once it was already in progress. As darkness fell, the SAS went into action in ten armoured vehicles packed with soldiers. On arrival, the tanks bulldozed through the perimeter wall, smashing outbuildings and cars as they did so.

The SAS, having learnt that the captured SAS had been moved from Jamiat to a house round the corner, changed their plans accordingly. They found the house, blew down the door and windows and stormed in, finding no resistance. The two captured SAS soldiers were found in a locked room. The belief was that dickers, the name given for local spies – the actual name 'dickers' originating from the war against the IRA in Ireland. These dickers had probably tipped the kidnappers off to the presence of the SAS. They had fled rather than be killed in a fire fight. The SAS suffered no serious injuries during the raid. However, the Iraqi police demanded compensation, furious that 100 prisoners had escaped and the police station had suffered damage. This corruption and underlying distrust is still evident in Iraq today and another barrier that hampers the war against IS.

Another issue with IS, is the weapons they have captured and began to use effectively. They are known to have Soviet, Polish and Bulgarian ZU23-2 and ZU23-4, towed anti-aircraft guns. Along with American low altitude FIM92 Stinger, shoulder mounted anti-aircraft systems. They have used DShK heavy-machine guns against the regime's dwindling force of attack helicopters to great effect, although they are not of much use against high-flying fast jets. These have been augmented, it is believed, by Chinese FN-6 portable missile systems which can hit targets at 11,000 feet and the earlier SA-16 Gimlet replaced by the (SA-18) which can hit targets at 16,000 feet, which had been supplied in large quantities to Bashar al-Assad's regime and then seized by IS fighters. They also have, the more powerful SA-24 portable air defence system, which is a more powerful version of the SA-16/18 and in service since 2004. Best estimates of around 250-350 missiles, but this could be much higher as in Syria alone the Assad regime had 20,000 portable missile launchers. IS has even seized a couple of M1 Abrahams tanks, although it is unlikely they have the spares and full technical expertise to maintain these complex turbine powered tanks.

One big issue is that the Syrian rebels have been receiving weapons funded by states in the Gulf. In late 2012 and early 2013, no less than 3,000 tonnes of former Warsaw Pact stock were shifted from Croatia to Syria via Jordan. The consignment was bankrolled by the Saudis, but they and other backers of the opposition, such as Qatar, are supposed to have desisted from supplying anti-aircraft missiles at the insistence of the Americans. However, according to unconfirmed reports from the Middle-East, the Saudis have offered to supply some rebel groups, not IS, with Chinese manpads. These rebels have turned out in the main to be fanatical IS fighters and many weapon supplies have been sent to Iraq to support the Iraqi operation as well. Any war needs munitions and this is still in plentiful supply by seizing existing supplies in Syria and Iraq.

Chapter Six – Close Call

Northern Iraq 0600 hrs

The early morning sunshine glinted off the bonnet of our 'borrowed' pickup truck. We were dressed in dish-dashes to look like locals on a Sunday morning drive. It was a good way to recce the main roads and keep an eye on ISIS movements as we travelled to meet some Iraqi soldiers. For the time and day there was quite a bit of traffic. Many were still trying to flee from where ISIS had control. We had heard of stories of young girls being held captive to satisfy sexual needs, further adding to the atrocities that IS have undertaken. One more reason to get rid of them, Deko wanted them all lined up and shot in the balls before shooting them in the head. The surprising part is the number of females that ISIS had recruited, some actively seeking out joining, to wage their so called holy war.

We travelled for miles before we saw a small ISIS patrol. We all had fingers on the triggers of our weapons hidden under our dish-dash. It was a tense moment, but we both drove on by. Scott noted down the number of them, direction of travel and number plates and description of the vehicle. If they had clocked us, it would have been an intense firefight. They out gunned us with an RPG, heavy machine gun and usual AK47s. We must have blended in well, as our suntan, was now about the same as the locals, with full beards further disguising our identities.

We carried on our travels filling up at a local filling station before Deko threw the correct amount of money on the counter, in what looked like an old and battered service station. We were mingling in with Iraqi's going about their daily business - unaware that a bunch of hairy SAS were amongst them.

Back on the road we continued to travel east towards Mosul before going south to Samarra then onto highway 23. Either side of the road was quite desolate in places. We passed by the odd village and farm as the heat of the day built up. Night patrols along a road did not yield much, as IS did seem to prefer to be in bed rather than fight at night. For all their rhetoric they are not as tough as they make out. Aggressive and violent - but two days on the Brecon Beacons with a gale force wind and pouring rain, they would be crying out for their mummy. They are the quintessential school bully, who needs to be stood up to and taught a damn good lesson. One upside of IS, is that they are not big users of IEDs. Unlike the Taliban, who love IEDs. IEDs in Afghanistan accounted for 66% of coalition casualties. IS still likes its suicide bombers and booby traps though, and maybe when IS are removed, they will hang around infiltrating planting IEDs just like the Taliban. With airstrikes, being stepped up and the SAS, SBS, Delta and the SEALs finding targets - IS in Iraq at least, was taking a pummelling - slowly bit by bit, IS is being pushed back from their strongholds. The long term goal is to push them back and ensure the Iraqi military forces are strong enough to stop IS ever getting a grip on the country again.

An hour later, after leaving the service station, it was time to turn off the road and join up with some Iraqi forces. To pass on intel and support the preparation for an attack on Falluja, which is in the Iraqi province of Al Anbar, located roughly 43 miles west of Baghdad on the Euphrates River. We were then going to go out with an Iraqi patrol to recce Ramadi.

As we left the smooth main road the difference was noticeable as we were jolted and bounced around on a dirt track that snaked its way through some fields, in what is best described as arid countryside. It had a primeval beauty, though, and I had grown to like it. It was hot, but much better than freezing my bollocks off in Hereford. With this job at present, you certainly get plenty of sunshine. Although, I do miss home at times, as the mission in Syria and Iraq are both physically and mentally tiring. I was part of mobility troop, which can trace its roots back to deserts of Northern Africa during World War 2, when the SAS used American Jeeps to attack airfields in Libya. Driving and using Vickers machine guns mounted on them to shoot up parked plans and ammo stores. Mobility troop requires various skills, like getting heavily laden vehicles over all kinds of terrain, maintaining and repairing the vehicles. We all attended an extensive REME (Royal Electric Mechanical Engineers) training course to gain skills at maintaining vehicles. Navigation is another very important skill, especially in a featureless desert. We do have the use of GPS devices, but even then you cannot beat a map and navigating by the stars.

It was a good 2 hours' drive from the main road to the Iraqi soldiers' camp. They all seemed in good spirits and welcomed us with open arms. We were not far Jazira, a block of neighbourhoods north of the Euphrates and south of Highway 11, not to be confused with the desert area of the same name abutting Syria. The area is physically linked to similar ISIS "support zones" south of Falluja and stretching down to the Jurf as-Sakhar area in northern Babil Province. ISIS has been strident in its defence of its southern launchpads. One example of their vigorous defence was in al-Humayra, an Iraqi Army probe was decimated on April 20, 2014, by wire-guided anti-tank missiles, with the loss of an entire mixed platoon of T-62 tanks and MTLB (multipurpose light armoured tracked vehicle). ISIS forces have been known to use titanium-coated, armour-piercing ammunition in Dragonov sniper rifles to shoot out the engine blocks on a large number of Iraqi Hummers in an apparent effort to reduce Iraqi Security Force (ISF) mobility. When Iraqi security forces began searching for IS bomb workshops in late March 2014, a car bomb damaged the bridge linking Ramadi city to the al-Ta'mim suburb, the historic site for ISIS bomb making workshops in Ramadi. ISIS has invested significant numbers of suicide fighters to keep the fight going in Ramadi. It is an area they want to have an influence over, even if the chance of taking Ramadi is small.

Falluja however, has seen ISIS undertake a creeping takeover. Falluja is an insular town renowned for its rebelliousness and links to Salafism. ISIS's preferred tactics in Falluja throughout 2013 were to undertake drive-by shootings, under-vehicle bombings and car bombings of houses belonging to local leaders and police forces. The ISIS also targeted electrical generator operators, shopkeepers and clerics in a slow-building campaign of fundraising and influence-building.

Clashes in western Iraq began on December 30, 2013 when Iraqi security forces cleared up a Sunni protest camp in Ramadi. Tribal militias then fought against the Iraqi Army. After the Iraqi Army withdrew from Anbar province to cool the situation on 31 December, militants from ISIS occupied parts of the Iraqi cities of Fallujah and Ramadi, in the predominantly Sunni Al Anbar governorate. Following the arrival of IS, most tribal militias in Ramadi allied themselves with government forces to counter them. In early January 2014, most of the Falluja police force ceased wearing uniforms and police stations associated with former Hamas al-Iraq members were abandoned to ISIS looting. From January 3 onwards, ISIS patrols cruised Falluja city in captured police vehicles using megaphones to call police officers to repent. The federal government was initially willing to contain the ISIS within Falluja, rather than risk a political and military setback during the electoral and government formation processes. Although, that did not work as well as expected, as ISIS still managed to break through the cordon as ISIS was determined to launch strategic high-impact attacks toward Baghdad. ISIS has wanted a renewed battle of Baghdad, a city where the Sunni minority and its militias were roundly defeated and purged in many areas by Shi`a militias in 2006-2007.

Using a different approach, the ISIS also manipulated its on-off control of the regulating dams downstream of Falluja to flood the Euphrates delta from April 6 2014 onwards, causing extensive displacement of rural residents and threatening to flood metropolitan Baghdad. This gamble, alongside the well-publicized execution of Iraqi special forces, appear to have been designed to lure the Iraqi military into a hasty assault on Falluja, a potential spark for a wider Sunni Arab uprising against the government. This though, has been counted by US assistance with the fight against groups in this area, by speeding up supply of equipment to Iraq, including Hellfire missiles, Scan Eagle UAVs (Unmanned Aerial Vehicle), and Raven UAVs. Then from August 2014 began airstrikes against IS in Iraq to be followed by the RAF is already performing surveillance missions soon to be followed by airstrikes on ISIS positions as well.

All this lead to over five months of fighting between ISIS and government forces until June 25, 2014 when ISIS advanced towards the Haditha Dam, the second-largest in Iraq, and reached Burwana, on the eastern side of Haditha.

Near Jazira Iraq 0500 hrs

We have been using hand lunched Drones for a while now, initially in Afghanistan. They really are great bits of kit. When I first saw the P-100 Black Hornet Nano we use, I thought it was a kid's toy the Regiment had brought from Toys R Us as a Joke. The black plastic main rotor and tail blade looked like a child's toy, coupled with the plastic body, which looked like it had come straight out the box of an unpainted Airfix kit. The body colour apparently makes it very hard to see at high or low level. Developed by Prox Dynamics AS of Norway, the PD-100 UAV itself is measured around 10×2.5 cm and weighs 16g. It can fly for around 20 minutes with a classified range.

The UAV is controlled via a joystick with several buttons and what is best described as a tablet that gives a live feed of what the UAV is seeing, control is semi-auto via movement buttons and with one key press, it can be recalled and will fly automatically back to the operator. GPS is used to locate enemy positions or items of interest; these can then be used for airstrikes or to plan an attack. Everything will easily fit in your day sack for ease of transportation. The US is planning on using them and just want night vision capabilities and a compatible data link and better navigational capacity.

Today, we were going to work with an Iraqi detachment and use the PD-100 to spy on an IS position, pending an attack. Along with, training from the Regiment to help combat the threat of IS and re-take areas captured by IS. They are excellent soldiers and pick up on our pointers very fast; the issue is their will and motivation to fight. I have no doubt if equipped properly, they will be able to push IS back, with a little fire support from US fighter jocks.

We dressed ourselves in the same uniforms as the Iraqi's to better blend in and Deko went off and had a quick chat with the Officer leading the Iraqi's, to instruct him via an interpreter what the plan was and what he expected of the Iraqi's. The chat seemed quite animated from a distance, but knowing Deko, he was ensuring everything had gone in and there would be no 'fuck ups,' he had had a couple of bad experiences in Syria with some of the rebel forces nearly getting a couple of his patrol killed. There was no doubt, the missions in Syria and Iraq were fraught with danger - we were fighting extremists. If they knew exactly who we were and where we were, the prize of capturing and then almost certainly killing us on camera, before uploading to YouTube would be too hard to resist and a propaganda coup. But, then we would never say we were SAS, just normal soldiers or if in civies anything from oil workers to part of the media, reporting on the war. With the rise of IS there is no doubt our mission has changed. Our new aim is to "cut the head off the snake" by hitting the command structure of ISIS. As in Afghanistan the SBS were with us, we do say the B is for 'B team' and the A in SAS because we are the A team. But to be honest without their man power we would struggle to have enough men to cover all the ops cross the globe, especially during the second Iraq war and Afghanistan. Our 'B' team colleagues have proved their worth, though, they have even impressed Delta Force during three weeks in May and June 2005, three Delta Force operators had been killed on operations in Iraq. With Delta Force squadrons fielding only 30 to 40 operators, it was not long before injuries and deaths started to have an impact on their capability. The UK Special Forces were asked to assist, but help was initially refused and another squadron of Delta Force operators was flown in. However, Delta Force found itself so committed and the intelligence they had needed to be acted upon so urgently that the British Task Force Black in Bagdad was given the job.

Operation Marlborough was hastily put together and was to be undertaken by M Squadron, who was on their second tour of duty in Baghdad. It was the kind of operation that M Squadron had yearned for. There were some members of G Squadron SAS who helped out, but the bulk of the personnel involved were SBS. It was a hot and humid night as the Special Forces assembled for the operation. There was still quite a bit of tension between the SAS and SBS. M Squadron had been mauled in Iraq back in 2003, losing most of its vehicles and equipment. The SAS felt that the SBS were not up to the job and labelled them 'Tier 2 SF'. At the time the SBS was looking to double in size, adding to the tension with the SAS. The SBS undertook the same joint selection process and many recruits had been syphoned off into the growing SBS. The SBS, though, was thought to have less macho swagger and more thoughtfulness than the SAS. Back in 2004, C Squadron had mounted 22 raids compared to the 85 raids A Squadron mounted in their tour in 2003. This made the SBS look laid-back and less able, even though in reality that was not the case. At that point it was down to the UK-US cooperation, where US SF would often get more and bigger operations and British SF would at times be side lined.

The team for Operation Marlborough consisted of 16 mainly SBS soldiers, including four SBS sniper teams, each armed with .338 Lapua

Magnum chambered L115A AWM sniper rifles. Escape routes were watched by the remaining members of the group in case of immediate emergency or escape if and when needed. The sniper team's mission was to kill Al-Qaeda terrorists wearing suicide vests laden with explosives. They later planned to detonate these vests in densely packed cafes and restaurants frequented by members of the Iraqi security forces. This intelligence had been obtained by Iraqi double agents working for both the British and US Secret Intelligence Services.

On 23 July 2005, the SBS arrived close to their target house, labelled Alpha, with a combination of Humvees and Puma helicopters. US personnel were also closely involved, with a detachment of Rangers acting as a backup force. Some M1 tanks had also been brought in as backup as the operation was in a dangerous neighbourhood. Overhead Task Force Black had Puma helicopters circling, carrying snipers in case the occupants of Alpha tried to launch an attack. A United States predator UAV circled above and had the target building under video surveillance, sending its imagery back to the Task Force Black Headquarters. Listening devices had already been laid inside the building and were being monitored by Arabic-speaking translators. Finally, a command and control aircraft also orbited ahead, linking all the various forces together through a single command. As the SBS moved forward towards their target, a man wearing a suicide vest came running out at them. He detonated his bomb, but it was too early to kill any of the SBS who had quickly taken cover and were crouching down when the vest detonated. The blast caused one of the Pumas that were circling about 100 feet above to rise up in the blast wave before dropping like a stone, trying to find some good air. The pilot, even at the low altitude the helicopter was at, managed to recover by winding up the engines to max power, and he started to pull up within feet of a rooftop. There was no time to dwell as the operation was picking up pace. Another of the airborne platforms had picked up via its image-intensifying camera a man leaving the back of a building and making a run for it. The circling Puma swung round to give the SBS sniper a chance to line up a shot. He lined him up in his sights before squeezing off a round that killed the man instantly. He was subsequently found to be another suicide bomber.

Alpha was now ready to be stormed by the SBS, who burst through the front door and conducted room by room clearance. As they went in, another man wearing a suicide vest ran towards them. One of the SBS opened up on him at close range, dropping him. He had been shot down before he had a chance to activate the bomb and lay slumped up against a blood-splattered wall. The SBS slowly made their way with a little trepidation, fearing that another suicide bomber may make another run for them. This time they may not be quite so lucky. Many of the rooms contained bomb parts and explosives, which meant a grenade, could not be thrown in for fear of setting all the explosives off. It was a slow process and no further suicide bombers were found. The SBS withdrew and the bomb disposal experts moved in. The SBS was commended for experiencing what Delta Force operatives had been experiencing as they hunted down Al-Qaeda cells.

The Puma helicopter pilot who had shown expert airmanship and rescued his bird was decorated for his airmanship. The SBS had proven that they were just as good as the SAS and Delta Force when taking on Al-Qaeda and prior to Operation Malbourough proved themselves during the Battle for Qala-i-Janghi in November 2001 when an eight man SBS team took on 600 Taliban fighters who were trying to revolt at the Qala-i-Janghi prison.

With us all kitted up and ready to go, the four of us mingled in with the Iraqi soldiers and began our patrol to Amirli, to scout out the area in advance of an attack by the Iraqi military. ISIS took Amirli in the Salah ad Din Governorate on June 11, 2014. It is in Northern Iraq and about 100 km from the Iranian border. Since ISIS has taken control the town has lacked access to food, electricity, and water. Most of the 26,000 residents are Shia Turkmen, who have organized local self-defence militias to fight against ISIS.

We needed to gather some intel on one area of Amirli, finding out guard positions and looking for potential routes for an attack. We needed to find any weak points the Iraqi's could exploit on their attack. We moved out in Iraqi military vehicles for the drive to Amirli mainly off road, before dismounting about a mile away and moving up on foot to get within range of the drones. The Iraqi's military job was to offer us all round defence so we could get on with launching drones. King was going to fly the drones whilst the rest of the patrol ensure security and kept the Iraqi soldiers on their toes. King had been on a course to learn how to fly the 'toy helicopter.' King had two drones stored in a plastic pouch clipped onto the top of the main tablet that acted as a viewing screen. It only took a matter of minutes to get the PD-100 UAV ready to go and King launched it from his hand, flying towards Amirli and an identified ISIS position, the idea was to fly in and recce the area around, looking for weak points and confirming the size and weapons the ISIS had. This up to date intel would aid the Iraq enormously with planning their attack. The PD-100 UAV quickly made it over the area to be recce'd, before starting a sweep and picking up some ISIS fighters and a BTR 80 armoured vehicle, we also found they had a T-62 along with a variety of light and heavy weapons that were easy for us to spot.

The vehicles were ripe for an airstrike, which we would put through, once we were out of the area. Airstrikes have been great at removing heavy armour and some of the heavy weapons that ISIS has seized from the Iraqi military and security forces as it has captured various areas of Iraq. With all the intel captured and sent to RHQ, it was time to mount up and get back to the Iraqi base. We would spend the next couple of days with the Iraqi military, undertaking some training and helping develop tactics to counter ISIS. At the end of those couple of days we would take our trusty Pickup back up towards Mosul and continue with some further hit and run raids ad pin pointing targets for Airstrikes.

CHAPTER EIGHT - JIHAD

The original meaning of jihad in Arabic is literally "struggle" is an Islamic term, which is a religious duty of Muslims. A person engaged in jihad is called a mujahid; the plural is mujahedeen, the term used for multi-national insurgent groups fighting against the Soviet's in Afghanistan from 1979 to the Soviet withdrawal in 1989. The word jihad appears frequently in the Quran, often in the idiomatic expression "striving in the way of God." In Shia Islam Jihad is one of the ten Practices of the Religion. However, Jihad is often translated into "holy war." If military jihad is required to protect the Muslim faith against others, it can be performed using anything from legal, diplomatic and economic to political means. If there is no peaceful alternative, Islam also allows the use of force, but there are strict rules of engagement. Innocent people such as women, children, or invalids - must never be harmed, and any peaceful offers to stop any further bloodshed from the enemy must be accepted.

Military action is therefore only one means of jihad, and is very rare. To highlight this point, the Prophet Mohammed told his followers returning from a military campaign: "This day we have returned from the minor jihad to the major jihad," which he said meant returning from armed battle to the peaceful battle for self-control and betterment. If military action appears necessary, not everyone can declare jihad. A religious, military campaign has to be declared by a proper authority, advised by scholars, who say the religion and people are under threat and violence is imperative to defend them. The concept of "a just war" is very important.

The concept of jihad has been hijacked by many political and religious groups over the ages in a bid to justify various forms of violence. In most cases, Islamic splinter groups invoked jihad to fight against the established Islamic order. Many scholars state that this misuse of the term jihad contradicts Islam.

Examples of sanctioned military jihad include the Muslims' defensive battles against the Crusaders in medieval times. What ISIS is doing, goes against any ideologies and is in effect a distorted version of religious beliefs to justify killing all non-believers, not just in Syria and Iraq but across the globe as well. Part of this jihad existence goes hand in hand with the adoption of a strict Muslim regime following Sharia law. Sharia law in Arabic means the moral code and religious law of a prophetic religion. The introduction of sharia is a longstanding goal for Islamist movements globally, including its introduction into Western countries, but attempts to impose sharia have been accompanied by controversy, violence, and even warfare.

True Sharia law, does not work very well with all western views or values. According to scholars of traditional Islamic law, the applicable rules for religious conversion under Sharia are as follows:

If a person converts to Islam, or is born and raised as a Muslim, then he or she will have full rights of citizenship in an Islamic state.

Leaving Islam is a sin and a religious crime. Once any man or woman is officially classified as Muslim, because of birth or religious conversion, he or she will be subject to the death penalty if he or she becomes an apostate, that is, abandons his or her faith in

Islam in order to become an atheist, agnostic or to convert to another religion. Before executing the death penalty, Sharia demands that the individual be offered one chance to return to Islam.

If a person has never been a Muslim, and is not a kafir (infidel, unbeliever), he or she can live in an Islamic state by accepting to be a dhimmi, or under a special permission called aman. As a dhimmi or under aman, he or she will suffer certain limitations of rights as a subject of an Islamic state, and will not enjoy complete legal equality with Muslims.

If a person has never been a Muslim, and is a kafir (infidel, unbeliever), Sharia demands that he or she should be offered the choice to convert to Islam and become a Muslim; if they reject the offer, he or she may either be killed, enslaved, or ransomed if captured.

It is the above laws, which ISIS has applied to the various religious sects, in particular Christians it has come across. With those refusing to convert being killed, in some circumstances whole villages and towns have been killed for refusing to convert. However, it is these continuing killings that have eventually led to small scale intervention to protect the local populous from harm. ISIS has fought back by murdering so far, two American and two British citizens, who have been beheaded in propaganda videos, warning about America's and the UK's intervention and attacks on ISIS.

An educated British jihadi nicknamed 'John' has become one of the world's most wanted man; after the beheading of US journalist James Foley. James Foley was captured in Syria in 2012. Foley was kidnapped by an organized gang after departing from an internet café in Binesh with his translator, in northwestern Syria on his way to the Turkish border on November 22, 2012, the translator was later released. At one point it was believed he had been kidnapped by Shabiha militia, a group loyal to Syrian President Bashar Assad, and he was held in a Syrian Air Force Intelligence complex in Damascus. Foley's captors demanded 100 million euros in ransom from Foley's family, GlobalPost, his employer, and the US for his release during negotiations from November to December 2013. GlobalPost spent millions trying to get James Foley released. They used a private security firm to help locate Foely. In September 2013 the firm was able to locate Foley and had been able to follow his locations. He had moved many times during his captivity. On 4 July 2014, just after midnight, U.S. air strikes were conducted against the ISIS military base known as the "Osama bin Laden Camp". Running in parallel and at almost the same time, 24 Delta Force members parachuted from helicopters near an ISIS building next to high value prisoners. These prisoners were believed to include James Foley, Steven Soltoff and Peter Kassig. The U.S. President had authorised a rescue operation for the prisoners. After landing the operators, blocked the main road towards Ar-Raqqah and began an assault on the prison. However, no prisoners were found in the building. Not wanting to come up empty handed the Delta operators decided instead to conduct house to house searches in Uqayrishah. Alerted to their presence ISIS forces began to arrive in the area and the Delta operators were now locked in a three hour firefight. Air support was brought in to stop Delta being overrun, ISIS tried to shoot down aircraft with RPGs but to no avail. During the firefight five ISIS militants were killed and one Delta operator wounded. No prisoners had been found and the only option was to abandon the operation. It was later found that the prisoners had been in the area, but had been moved 24 hours earlier. On August 12, 2014, Foley's parents received an email from his captors taking issue with the US government, saying it had refused to pay ransoms, unlike other governments, refused to negotiate prisoner exchanges, and "had no motivation to deal with the Muslims except through force". The email's then went on to say that they had left the US alone since its "disgraceful defeat in Iraq," and they would avenge the US bombing sin Iraq with the death of Foley. Foley's whereabouts were unknown to most until August 19, 2014, when ISIS uploaded a video to YouTube entitled "A Message to America". The video was quickly removed and showed Foley alive and then after he had been decapitated, with the corpse being shown. One Britsh Jihadist was identified by Mi6 and Mi5 as 23-year-old British former rapper, Abdel-Majed Abdel Bary was originally named as "Jihadi John," but later ruled out.

On the 26 February 2015, Jihadi John in various videos depicting beheadings, was announced by security agencies as 27 year old Mohammed Emwazi, from west London. His close friends stated that he was the ISIS executioner-in-chief. Mohammed was the son of a cab driver. He moved to the UK from Kuwait aged six and lived with his parents and three siblings in a Queen's Park council flat in London.

Along with others, Mohammed was involved in the execution of a second American-Israeli journalist Steven Sotloff. Sotloff was executed in the same manner as Foley. On 2 September 2014, ISIS released a video depicting Sotloff's execution, at the same time a British hostage David Haine was also shown and said to be next as retribution for military action and a call to halt military action by the US and UK. Sotloff had been kidnapped in Aleppo, Syria, on August 4, 2013. David Haines was then executed and another British citizen Alan Henning could be next. MI5 along with the CIA have worked hard in the background to collect intelligence and try to unmask the executioner and pinpoint his location so Special Forces can do their bit. MI5 (Military Intelligence, Section 5), is the UKs domestic counterintelligence and security agency and is part of its intelligence machinery alongside the Secret Intelligence Service (SISIS; also known as MI6) focused on foreign threats.

The killer was identified as being from London's East End due to his accent and the leader of a murderous team of UK-born militants dubbed "The Beatles" by captives due to being British.

Having advertised his laptop on classified adverts website Gumtree, he went to meet a prospective buyer at Maida Vale underground station near his West London home.

He wrote, ungrammatically: "*When I sell anything via internet i always only write my surname in the ad... I went to meet that person... so that he could have a look at the laptop & if it satisfied him then he would buy it...*

'That person to my surprise didn't even bother looking to see of the laptop works or not!!! (when you buy something, from someone you've never seen before you most likely would test the product!!)...

'Anyway, in a matter of seconds, I gave him the laptop (thinking that hes going to test the laptop) & he gave me the money straight-away... We "shacked hands" & he said "nice doing business with you Mohammed". I NEVER TOLD THIS PERSON MY FIRST NAME!! & I NEVER GIVE OUT MY FIRST NAME!! IT WAS IMPOSSIBLE FOR HIM TO KNOW MY FIRST NAME!!'

He added: 'I felt shocked, & paused for a few seconds as he walked away... I knew it was them!! Sometimes i feel like im a dead man walking, not fearing they may kill me.

'Rather, fearing that one day, I'll take as many pills as I can so that I can sleep for ever!! I just want to get away from these people!!!'

During the rally, which attracted at least 1,500 people, Michael Adebolajo spoke to the crowd of his contempt for 'unbelievers'. Adebolajo – who is in prison for Rigby's murder – said: 'They are pigs. Allah says they are worse than cattle. Do not be scared of them. And do not turn your back to them. Don't be scared of them, or police, or the cameras." Source: Daily Mail

Mohammed was a member of a 'sleeper' cell dubbed The London Boys, which included three operatives allegedly trained at an Al Qaeda camp in Somalia. All three were close associates of Emwazi. Until now, Emwazi was thought only to have been a peripheral figure among the capital's Islamic extremists. Yet a court document seen by this newspaper alleges that he was closely involved in the cell's activities, including the 'provision of funds and equipment to Somalia... for terrorism related activity'.

Before his death, Bin Laden sent 'angry' messages from his Pakistan hideout urging those returning from training to carry out attacks.

Inevitably, the depth of Emwazi's involvement in extremism – during a period when he was being monitored by MI5 – will increase pressure on security chiefs, who have faced criticism for failing to stop him joining ISIS in Syria.

The father of Mohammed was a police officer in Kuwait before the family moved to Britain, according to a former friend. Jasem Emwazi took his wife, children and eldest son Mohammed, then six, to start a new life in London in 1994. Meanwhile, a senior Kuwaiti military source suggested that, in common with many of his Bedoon ethnic group who originally stemmed from Southern Iraq, Mr Emwazi would have found it difficult to regain his police job in Kuwait following the Iraqi invasion of Kuwait and the 1991 Gulf War. Many Bedoon joined the Kuwaiti police and military in the 70s and 80s, even though they were not citizens of Kuwait. A recently retired Kuwait army colonel Fahad Al-Shilaimi stated that many of the stateless Bedoon were sacked from the police in the early 1990s. In the days after Saddam's men left, anyone with a link to Iraq found their loyalty questioned, and many were sacked. This may be the reason that the Emwazi family left Kuwait. Was this the initial seed that started Mohammed down the hate path years later, and would change a perfectly normal and pleasant young man, into someone filled with hatred for the west?

Other members of Mohammed's cell include Ibrahim Magag, a Somali-born former train conductor from London involved in arranging 'financial support for Al Qaeda'. Magag was put under a control order to stop him fleeing overseas to join a jihad. But on Boxing Day 2012 he vanished. Officials believe he went to join British jihadis in East Africa.

A British Journalist Richard Verkaik met Mohammed 'Jihadi John' before he left for Syria. *"Like many young Muslim men at the time, he appeared to have a grievance. But this man was different – in him was a warped sense of injustice that could never justify the barbaric acts of murder that he has gone on to carry out in Syria. He seemed to have a persecution complex and desperately wanted his story to be told. When he sold his laptop on the internet, he was convinced it had been purchased by the security services. His concerns seemed to border on paranoia. He sent me the complaint that he had submitted to the Independent Police Complaints Commission setting out his allegations against police officers when he was held at Heathrow after returning from Kuwait earlier in the year. Throughout all our dealings, he was polite and appeared to understand the pressures of journalism. But he refused to provide a picture to accompany the story and we lost contact."*

As early as January 2007 three of Mohammed's associates - CE, Mohammed Ezzouek and Hamza Chentouf found themselves among a refugee convoy fleeing Somalia after US air strikes on Islamists who had seized Mogadishu. It was reported that they were captured by SAS soldiers across the border in Kenya and handed to its authorities for questioning. The Britons ended up being sent back to Somalia, before a plane was chartered to airlift them out at an estimated cost of £50,000. Both Ezzouek and Chentouf, who deny terrorism, claimed they were innocents abroad in the wrong place at the wrong time. Mohammed at the time was close to a gang called the 'London Boys' which robbed wealthy residents on the streets of Belgravia, Central London, using stun guns. Two of the gang were believed to have later travelled to Syria a year before Mohammed, and were subsequently killed. This may have led to Mohammed wanting to take up arms and avenge his fallen 'brothers' further feeding his hatred.

One ex-captive described Jihadi John as intelligent, educated and a devout believer in radical Islamic teachings. A linguistics expert at the University of York a Prof Paul Kerswill, thought the executioner spoke in "multicultural London English" usually found in the East End before he was identified as Mohammed Emwazi. He said, "He probably has a foreign language background, but it sounds like multicultural London English, which is people from all kinds of backgrounds who mix in the East End, a new cockney." It was then the job of the regiment to then hunt Mohammed down and arrest him, although it would be more than likely that we would have to kill him, as there would be no way Mohammed would come quietly. As we were 'out an about' any British ISIS we managed to capture, dead or alive would be identified by Biometrics, as MI5 managed to uncover a potential identity the Regiment would be tasked with going in and getting him. Although, it was more than likely Mohammed was in Syria as opposed to Iraq. The location of the execution videos has been identified as being filmed in Syria. To me these British Jihadists had committed treason against their own country. It is not for me to decide what the best course of action is with them, which is down to the politicians who fight a battle with world leaders on deciding how far we should intervene. The SAS is just another tool they can use, although I think of us as a surgical tool to cut out the cancer that no one else dares to do, or is reluctant to do. In this case it is ISIS which is a cancer that is spreading quickly. We can cut out parts, put a longer term solution is needed to get rid of ISIS permanently. Extremists will always be present, wanting to force their ideology on the world or simply get rid of a government. Countries, governments and individuals need to stand firm and not allow them to get a grip. We do seem to be descending into a more violent period; those with gloom on their side feel it is a precursor to another world war. Personally, I see it as a few more madmen than usual, exploiting countries that are in turmoil and using it to gain money and power. But, how a seemingly pleasant young man such as Mohammed are turned into hate filled monsters is something we need to address. Those that spread hate, are most certainly behind so much indoctrination and changing a person's belief to the point that they will freely kill for what they believe in.

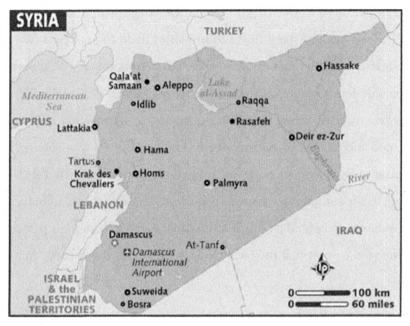

Syrian Civil War March 2011 – March 2013

The Syrian Civil War, also known as the Syrian Uprising, is an ongoing armed conflict which ISIS have now entered. The unrest that was essentially the build-up began in the early spring of 2011 with nationwide protests against President Bashar al-Assad's government, whose forces responded with violent crackdowns. Syria ha borders with Iraq, Turkey, Israel and the Lebanon. Syria covers an area of 71,479 sq mi and an estimated population of 17,951,639. The modern day Syrian state was established after World War I as a French mandate, and represented the largest Arab state to emerge from the formerly Ottoman-ruled Arab Levant. It gained independence in April 1946, as a parliamentary republic. The name "Syria" was formerly synonymous with the Levant (known in Arabic as al-Sham).

Syria consists mostly of arid plateau, although the northwest is the fairly green part of the country borders the Mediterranean. The Northeast of the country known as "Al Jazira" and in the South "Hawran" are important agricultural areas. The Euphrates River (flows through Iraq as well), Syria's most important river, crosses the country in the east.

The climate in Syria is hot and dry. Syrian winters are mild, although due to the country's elevation, snowfall does occasionally occur during winter. Petroleum in commercial quantities was first discovered in the northeast in 1956. The most important oil fields are those of Suwaydiyah, Qaratshui, Rumayian, and Tayyem, near Dayr az–Zawr. The fields are a natural extension of the Iraqi fields of Mosul and Kirkuk. Petroleum became Syria's leading natural resource and chief export after 1974. Natural gas was discovered at the field of Jbessa in 1940.

Syria became an independent republic in 1946, although democratic rule was ended by a CIA-supported coup in March 1949, followed by two more coups that year. An uprising against military rule in 1954 saw the army transfer power to civilians; from 1958 to 1961, a brief union with Egypt replaced Syria's parliamentary system with a highly centralized presidential regime. The Ba'ath Syrian Regional Branch government came to power in 1963 after a successful coup d'état. In 1966, another coup overthrew the traditional leaders of the party, Michel Aflaq and Salah al-Din al-Bitar. General Hafez al-Assad, the Minister of Defence, seized power in a "corrective revolution" in November 1970, becoming Prime Minister. Then in March 1971, General Assad declared himself President, a position that he held until his death in 2000. Since then, the secular Syrian Regional Branch has remained the dominant political authority in what is virtually a single-party state in Syria; Syrian citizens may only approve the President by referendum and – until the government-controlled multi-party 2012 parliamentary election – could not vote in multi-party elections for the legislature.

Bashar al-Assad, the current President of Syria and Asma al-Assad, his wife – who is a British-born and British-educated Sunni Muslim, initially inspired hopes for democratic and state reforms and a "Damascus Spring" of intense social and political debate took place between July 2000 and August 2001. The period was characterized by the emergence of numerous political forums or salons, where groups of like-minded people met in private houses to debate political and social issues. Political activists such as Riad Seif, Haitham al-Maleh, Kamal al-Labwani, Riyad al-Turk and Aref Dalila were important in mobilizing the movement. The most famous of the forums, were the Riad Seif Forum and the Jamal al-Atassi Forum. The Damascus Spring ended in August 2001. With the arrest and imprisonment of ten leading activists who had called for democratic elections and a campaign of civil disobedience. From 2001 even reformists in Parliament had begun to criticize the legacy of stagnation since the rule of former President Hafez al-Assad; Bashar al-Assad has talked about reform, but carried out very little, and he has failed to deliver on promised reforms since 2000. This laid the foundations for the unrest that would simmer and eventually boil over into civil war.

Small protests began in Syria on 28 January 2011, before mass protests began on 15 March in Damascus and Aleppo, and spread across more cities, while growing in size in the following days. The week of 15–21 March is considered in many quarters to be the beginning of the Syrian uprising. On 18 March, the protests turned bloody when the Syrian government reacted with deadly violence. On 20 March in Daraa, after security forces opened fire on the protesting crowd, protesters burned the local Ba'ath Party headquarters, the town's courthouse and a telephone company building. That day 15 demonstrators and 7 policemen were killed in Daraa. By 25 March, 90 civilians and 7 policemen had been killed in Syria.

The protesters' demands up until 7 April had been predominantly democratic reforms, release of political prisoners, "freedom", abolition of emergency law and an end to corruption. After 8 April, the emphasis in demonstration slogans gradually shifted towards the call to overthrow the Assad government.

The protests spread across Syria and grew in intensity on Friday, 8 April, they occurred simultaneously in ten cities. By Friday, 22 April protests occurred in twenty cities. On 25 April, the Syrian Army started a series of large-scale military attacks on towns, using tanks, infantry carriers, and artillery, to try and curb the ever more violent protests, which lead to hundreds of civilians dying. By the end of May 2011, 1,000 civilians and 150 soldiers and policemen had been killed along with thousands having been detained. Among those arrested were many students, liberal activists and human rights advocates. Assad, in his March 2011 speech addressed the protests. He claimed that an international terrorist conspiracy sought to topple his government. During this time, Assad released extremists from the Sednaya prison; extremists with no association to the uprisings. These fighters would go on to lead militant groups such as ISIS and al-Qaeda affiliate Jabhat al Nusra.

Large scale armed rebellion against the state began on 4 June in Jisr al-Shugur, a city in Idlib Governorate near the Turkish border, after security forces on a post office roof had fired at a funeral demonstration. Protesting mourners, who were angry by the attack, set fire to the building, killing eight security officers, and then overran a police station, seizing weapons from it. Violence continued and escalated over the following days. More protesters in Syria began to take up arms. At the same time more soldiers defected to try to protect the protesters. By the end of July 2011, around 1,600 civilians and 500 security forces had been killed and 13,000 arrested.

On 29 July 2011, seven Syrian officer, who had defected, formed the Free Syrian Army (FSA) aiming "to bring this regime down" with united opposition forces. Composed of defected Syrian Armed Forces personnel and civilian volunteers, the rebel army sought to remove Bashar al-Assad and his government from power. The forming of the FSA marked the establishment of a rebel military resistance to the Assad government. The FSA grew in size, to about 20,000 by December 2011, and to an estimated 40,000 by June 2012. The real issue was that the group had remained without centralized leadership until December 2012. The FSA, along with other insurgent groups, relied mostly on light weapons, including assault rifles and rocket-propelled grenades. On 31 July, a nationwide crackdown nicknamed the "Ramadan Massacre" resulted in the death of at least 142 people and hundreds of injuries.

On 23 August, a coalition of anti-government groups was formed, the Syrian National Council. The group, based in Turkey, attempted to organize the opposition. However, the opposition, including the FSA, remained a fractious collection of political groups, longtime exiles, grass-roots organizers and armed militants, divided along ideological, ethnic or sectarian lines. Throughout August, Syrian forces entered major urban centres and outlying regions to attack protests. On 14 August, the Siege of Latakia continued as the Syrian Navy became involved in the military crackdown for the first time. Gunboats fired heavy machine guns at waterfront districts in Latakia, as ground troops and security agents backed by armour stormed several neighbourhoods.

By September 2011, organized units of Syrian rebels were engaged in an active insurgency campaign across Syria. A major confrontation between the FSA and the Syrian armed forces occurred in Rastan. From 27 September to 1 October, Syrian government forces, backed by tanks and helicopters, led a major offensive on the town of Al-Rastan in Homs Governorate, in order to drive out army defectors. After a week of intense and bloody fighting, the FSA was forced to retreat from Rastan. By October 2011, the FSA started to receive support from Turkey, who allowed the rebel army to operate its command and headquarters from the country's southern Hatay Governorate close to the Syrian border, and its field command from inside Syria. The FSA started to launch attacks into Syria's northern towns and cities, while using the Turkish side of the border as a safe zone and supply route. A year after its formation, the FSA gained control over many towns close to the Turkish border.

In October 2011, clashes between government and defected army units were being reported fairly regularly. During the first week of the month, clashes were reported in Jabal al-Zawiya in the mountainous regions of Idlib Governorate. Syrian rebels captured most of Idlib city as well. In mid-October, other clashes in Idlib Governorate include the city of Binnish and the town of Hass in the governorate near the mountain range of Jabal al-Zawiya. By late October, other clashes occurred in the northwestern town of Maarrat al-Nu'man in the governorate between government forces and defected soldiers at a roadblock on the edge of the town, and near the Turkish border, where 10 security agents and a deserter were killed in a bus ambush.

Clashes between the FSA and security forces in Homs escalated in early November as the siege continued. After six days of bombardment, the Syrian Army stormed the city, leading to heavy street fighting in several neighbourhoods. The Syrian Arm found resistance in Homs to be much greater than that seen in other towns and cities.

November and December 2011 saw increasing rebel attacks, as opposition forces grew in number. In the two months, the FSA launched deadly attacks on an air force intelligence complex in the Damascus suburb of Harasta, the Ba'ath Syrian Regional Branch youth headquarters in Idlib Governorate, Syrian Regional Branch offices in Damascus, an airbase in Homs Governorate, and an intelligence building in Idlib. Opposition fighters ambushed checkpoints and military bases around Daraa on December 15, killing 27 soldiers, in one of the largest attacks yet on security forces. The opposition then suffered a major setback on December 19, when a failed defection in Idlib governorate, lead to 72 defectors being killed.

In early January 2012, Assad began using large-scale artillery operations against the insurgency, which led to the destruction of many civilian homes due to indiscriminate shelling of civilian buildings and those thought to be occupied by insurgents. Daily protests had now been replaced with armed conflict. Intense clashes around the suburbs of Damascus, with the Syrian Army use of tanks and artillery becoming common. Fighting in Zabadani began on January 7 when the Syrian Army entered the town in an attempt to rout out FSA presence. After the first phase of the battle had ended with a ceasefire on January 18, leaving the FSA in control of the town, the FSA launched an offensive into nearby Douma. It lasted nine days before Januray 30; the rebels were forced to retreat from a government force counteroffensive. The Syrian Army managed to retake most of the suburbs, although with pockets of resistance. Fighting had erupted once again in Rastan on January 29, when soldiers, many checkpoints in Rastan started to fire on soldiers loyal to the government.

On February 3, the Syrian army launched a major offensive to retake rebel-held neighbourhoods. In early March, after weeks of artillery bombardments and heavy street fighting, the Syrian army eventually captured the district of Baba Amr, a major rebel stronghold. The Syrian Army also captured the district of Karm al-Zeitoun on March 9, where activists said that government forces killed 47 women and children. By the end of March, the Syrian army retook control of half a dozen districts, leaving them in control of 70 percent of the city.

81

In April 2011, Assad began employing attack helicopters against rebel forces. Then, on 12 April, the Syrian Government and rebels of the FSA ceasefire that had been mediated by the UN. It was a failure, with infractions of the ceasefire by both sides, resulting in several dozen casualties. Following the Houla massacre of May 25, 2012, where 108 people were executed in two separate incidents and the consequent FSA ultimatum to the Syrian government, the ceasefire practically collapsed, as the FSA began nationwide offensives against government troops. On 1 June, President Assad vowed to crush the anti-government uprising, after the FSA announced that it was resuming "defensive operations". On 5 June, fighting broke out in Haffa and nearby villages in the coastal governorate of Latakia Governorate. Rebels fought with government forces backed by helicopter gunships in the heaviest clashes in the governorate since the revolt began. Syrian forces seized the territory from rebels following eight days of fighting and shelling. On 6 June 78 civilians were killed in the Al-Qubeir massacre. According to activist sources, government forces started by shelling the village before the Shabiha militia moved in. On the June 12, the UN officially announced that Syria was in a state of Civil War. The peace plan practically collapsed by early June and the UN mission was withdrawn from Syria. Annan officially resigned from the UN in frustration on August 2, 2012.

The conflict began to move into the two largest cities, Damascus and Aleppo, which the government had said were dominated by a pro-Assad silent majority. On June 22, a Turkish RF-4E phantom jet fighter was shot down by Syrian air defences, whilst in international airspace near the Turkey/Syrian border, killing both pilots. Tensions between Syria and Turkey dramatically escalated following this incident, as both sides disputed whether the jet had been flying in Syrian or international airspace when it was shot down. Despite Turkish Prime Minister Recep Tayyip Erdoğan's vows to retaliate harshly against Assad's government, no such intervention materialised. Bashar al-Assad publicly apologised for the incident, and relations between the two countries cooled. By July 10, rebel forces had captured most of the city of Al-Qusayr, in Homs Governorate, after weeks of fighting. By mid-July, the rebels had captured the town of Saraqeb, in Idlib Governorate. With fighting, spreading across the country and 16,000 people killed, the International Committee of the Red Cross declared the conflict a civil war. Fighting in Damascus intensified, with a major rebel push to take the city.

Then in late July, government forces managed to break the rebel offensive on Damascus by pushing out most of the opposition fighters, although fighting still continued on the outskirts. In August, 2012 the government began using fixed-wing warplanes against the rebels.

On July 19, Iraqi officials reported that the FSA had gained control of all four border checkpoints between Syria and Iraq. In late September, the FSA moved its command headquarters from southern Turkey into rebel-controlled areas of northern Syria. By October 18, the FSA had captured Douma, the biggest suburb of Damascus

After Brahimi's ceasefire agreement for Eid, officially ended on October 30, the Syrian military expanded its aerial bombing campaign in Damascus. A bombing of the Damascus district of Jobar was the first instance of a fighter jet being used in Damascus airspace to attack targets in the city. In early November 2012, rebels made significant gains in northern Syria. The rebel capture of Saraqib in Idlib governorate, which lies on the strategic M5 highway, further isolated Aleppo from government-controlled areas of the country. The problem was that the rebels lack anti-aircraft weapons to halt helicopter and fixed wing ground attacks. On November 3, rebels launched an attack on the Taftanaz air base, a core base for the Syrian military helicopter and bombing operations. The rebels then took control of Base 46 in the Aleppo Governorate on November 18. Base 46 in Norther Syria, was one of the Syria Army's largest bases. It had taken six weeks to capture with 300 Syrian soldiers dead. With the capture of the base came the capture of large amounts of heavy armour along with munitions. Mayadeen military base in the country's eastern Deir ez-Zor Governorate was also captured on November 22.

In mid-December 2012, American officials stated that the Syrian military had resorted to firing Scud ballistic missiles at rebel fighters inside Syria. It was reported that, six Scud missiles were fired at the Sheikh Suleiman base north of Aleppo, which rebel forces had occupied. Later on in December, a further Scud attack took place near Marea, a town in a rebel-held area north of Aleppo near the Turkish border. In late December, rebel forces pushed further into Damascus, taking control of the adjoining Yarmouk and Palestine refugee camps, pushing out pro-government Popular Front for the Liberation of Palestine-General Command fighters with the help of other factions. Rebel forces launched an offensive against army positions in Hama governorate. Rebel forces also captured the northern town of Harem near the Turkish border in Idlib governorate, after weeks of heavy fighting.

On January11, 2013, Islamist groups, including al-Nusra Front, took full control of the strategic Taftanaz air base in the northern Idlib governorate, after weeks of fighting. The air base, one of the largest in northern Syria, was often used by the military to carry out helicopter raids and deliver supplies. The rebels were able to seize helicopters, rocket launchers and other weapons.

On 11 February, Islamist rebels captured the town of Al-Thawrah in Ar-Raqqah Governorate and the nearby Tabqa Dam, Syria's largest dam and a key source of hydroelectricity. The next day, rebel forces took control of Jarrah air base, located 60 kilometres (37 mi) east of Aleppo. The base had been used to launch bombing raids in Aleppo governorate, and had served as an important supply line for the Assad government. On 14 February, fighters from al-Nusra Front took control of Shadadeh, a town located in Al-Hasakah Governorate near the Iraqi border. On February 21, the FSA in Quasar began shelling Hezbollah positions in Lebanon. Prior to this, Hezbollah militants had been shelling villages near Quasar from within Lebanon. A 48-hour ultimatum was issued by an FSA commander on February 20, warning the militant group to stop the attacks or face retaliation. The rebels had managed to capture parts of Raqqa but not capture it outright. On March 4, rebel forces launched an offensive to capture Raqqa outright. By March 6, the rebels had captured the entire city, effectively making Raqqa the first provincial capital to be lost by the Assad government. Residents of Raqqa celebrated by toppling a bronze statue of his late father Hafez Assad in the centre of the city. The rebels also seized two top government officials.

On March 18, the Syrian Air Force attacked rebel positions in Lebanon for the first time. The attack occurred at the Wadi al-Khayl Valley area, near the border town of Arsal. On 23 March, several rebel groups seized the 38th division air defense base in southern Daraa governorate near a strategic highway linking Damascus to Jordan. The very next day, rebels captured a 25 km strip of land near the Jordanian border, which included the towns of Muzrib, Abdin, and the al-Rai military checkpoint.

Then on March 25, rebels launched one of their heaviest bombardments of Central Damascus since the revolt began. Beginning in Kafr Souseh district, mortars reached Umayyad Square, where the Ba'ath Party headquarters, Air Force Intelligence and state television are located. On 29 March, rebels captured the strategic town of Da'el after days of fierce fighting. The town is located in Daraa Governorate, along the strategic highway connecting Damascus to Jordan. On 3 April, rebels captured a military base near the city of Daraa.

CHAPTER TEN – CIVIL WAR

Syrian Civil War April 2013 – August 2014

Government forces in Syria managed to breach a six month, rebel blockade in Wadi al-Deif, near Idlib on April 17, 2013. Heavy fighting was also reported around the town of Babuleen after government troops outflanked weakened rebel positions with troops attempting to secure control of a main highway leading to Aleppo. The break in the siege also allowed government forces to resupply two major military bases in the region, which had been relying on sporadic airdrops and in need of more substantial re-supply. On April 18, the FSA took control of Al-Dab'a Air Base near the city of al-Qusayr. The base had no aircraft and was being used primarily to garrison Syrian ground troops. Meanwhile, the Syrian Army re-captured the town of Abel. The SOHR director described the loss of the town by saying that it will hamper rebel movements between al-Qusayr and Homs city. According to him, the capture of the airport would have relieved the pressure on the rebels in the area, but their loss of Abel made the situation more complicated. The same day, the rebels reportedly assassinated Ali Ballan, who was head of public relations at the Ministry of Social Affairs and a member of Syria's relief agency, in a restaurant at Mazzeh district in Damascus.

On April 21, pro-Assad forces captured the towns of Burhaniya, Saqraja and al-Radwaniya near the Lebanese border. After five weeks of fighting, government troops re-took control of the town of Otaiba, east of Damascus on April 25. Otabia had been under rebel control for the previous eight months, serving as the main arms supply route from

Jordan. On 2 May, government forces captured the town of Qaysa in a steady push north from the city's airport. Troops also retook the Wadi al-Sayeh central district of Homs, driving a wedge between two rebel strongholds.

On 8 May, government forces captured the strategic town of Khirbet Ghazaleh, situated along the highway to the Jordanian border. Over 1,000 rebel fighters withdrew from the town due to the lack of reinforcements and ammunition. The loss of the town also resulted in the reopening of the government supply-route to the contested city of Daraa. The rebels continued to withdraw from other towns so as to not face the Army's advance along the highway. On May 11, the rebels managed to cut a newly built road across the desert, used as an Army supply route between central Syria and Aleppo's airport. On May 12, government forces took complete control of Khirbet Ghazaleh and secured the highway near the town.

On 13 May, government forces captured the towns of Western Dumayna, Haidariyeh, and Esh al-Warwar allowing them to block supplies to the rebels in al-Qusayr. Then from May 16, rebels stated that they recaptured the town of Al-Qisa after launching a unified counteroffensive and the next day the rebels captured four villages in Eastern Hama, including the Alawite town of Tulaysiah. The villages had been abandoned by its resident's days before the rebels arrived. The Syrian army then launched its offensive against the rebel-held town of Qusayr after taking control of surrounding villages and countryside.

The turning point of the offensive was reached when Hezbollah fighters took control of the Al Tal area overlooking Qusayr. On May

23, rebels captured a military base near the town of Nairab. By May 29, government forces captured the al-Dabaa air base, north of al-Qusayr. In the first two days of June after heavy fighting, the Syrian Army recaptured three of the Alawite villages that had been previously captured by the rebels in Eastern Hama governorate, after rebel forces retreated from the area. Rebel forces then withdrew from al-Qusayr on June 5, and the Syrian military and its allies took full control of the town. The following day, government forces captured the nearby village of Dabaa.

On June 7, Syrian troops backed by Hezbollah captured two villages north of al-Qusayr: Salhiyeh and Masoudiyeh. They captured the village of Buwaydah, the last rebel-held village in the al-Qusayr region the next day. Between June 7 and 14, Army troops, government militiamen, and Hezbollah fighters launched operations in Aleppo Governorate. Over a one-week period, government forces had advanced both in Aleppo city and the countryside around the city, pushing back the rebels. On June 10, Shia pro government fighters from the village of Hatla, east of Deir al-Zour, attacked a nearby rebel position, killing four rebels. In retaliation for the attack, the next day, thousands of rebels attacked and captured the village, killing 60 residents, fighters and civilians. On June 14, the Al Nusra front captured a military barracks near Idlib city, after three days of fighting. Then on June 15, the Syrian Army captured the Damascus suburb of Ahmadiyeh near the city's airport.

By the end of June, rebel forces had captured a major military checkpoint in the city of Daraa On 18 July, Kurdish YPG forces secured control of the northern town of Ras al-Ain, after days of fighting with the al-Nusra Front. In the following three months, continued fighting between Kurdish and mainly jihadist rebel forces led to the capture of two dozen towns and villages in Hasakah Governorate by Kurdish fighters, while the Jihadists made limited gains against the Kurds in Aleppo and Raqqah governorates after they turned on the Kurdish rebel group Jabhat al-Akrad over its relationship with the YPG. In Aleppo, Islamists "ethnically cleansed" Kurds from towns in the countryside by massacring them, leading to a mass migration of civilians to the town of Afrin. FSA fighters seized control of the western Aleppo suburb of Khan al-Asal on July 22. The town was the last government stronghold in the western portion of Aleppo governorate, and it was also located on a route linking Aleppo with the rest of the governorate.

On August 4, around 10 rebel brigades, backed by heavy weaponry, launched a large-scale offensive on the government stronghold of Latakia Governorate. Initial attacks by 2,000 opposition members seized as many as 12 villages in the mountainous area, taking advantage of the rugged terrain on August the 4 and 5. However, in mid-August, the military counterattacked and recaptured all of the territory previously lost to the rebels in the coastal region during the offensive.

On 6 August, rebels captured all of Menagh Military Airbase in northern Syria after a 10-month siege. The strategic airbase is located on the road between Aleppo city and the Turkish border. On 24 August, rebels captured the town of Ariha. However, after 10 days of bombardment, government forces recaptured Ariha on 3 September. On August 26, rebel forces took over the strategic town of Khanasir in Aleppo governorate which was the government's last supply route for the contested city of Aleppo. On September 8, rebels led by the al-Nusra Front captured the Christian town of Maaloula, 43 km north of Damascus. The Syrian Army launched a counterattack a few days later, recapturing the town.

On September 18, members of the Islamic State of Iraq and the Levant (ISIS) overran the FSA-held town of Azaz in the north of the country. The fighting was the most severe since tensions rose between militant factions in Syria earlier in the year. Soon after ISIS captured Azaz, a ceasefire was announced between the rival rebel groups. However, in early October, more fighting between rebels erupted in the town. In mid-September, the Syrian military captured the towns of Deir Salman and Shebaa on the outskirts of Damascus. The Army also captured six villages from opposition forces in eastern Homs.

The rebels seized the Ramtha border post in Daraa Governorate on the Syrian, Jordan crossing on September 28 after days of fighting which left 26 soldiers dead along with 7 foreign rebel fighters. On October 3, AFP reported that Syria's army re-took the strategic town of Khanasir, which is located on a key supply route linking central Syria to the city of Aleppo. Opposition forces had cut off the army's supply route to Aleppo when they seized the town and nearby villages in August. The rebels went on to seize Hajanar guard post on the Jordanian border near Daraa after a month of fierce fighting on October 9. Its fall meant rebels were now in control of a swath of territory along the border from outside of Daraa to the edge of Golan Heights.

The same day, Hezbollah and Iraqi Shiite fighters, backed up by artillery, air-strikes and tanks, attacked and captured the town of Sheikh

Omar, on the southern outskirts of Damascus. Two days later, the Lebanese and Iraqis also captured the towns of al-Thiabiya and Husseiniya on the southern approaches to Damascus. The capture of the three towns, located between the two main highways leading to Jordan, strengthened the government hold on major supply lines and put more pressure on rebels under siege in the Eastern Ghouta area.

The Syrian Army along with its allies, Hezbollah and the al-Abas brigade, launched an offensive on two key fronts, Damascus and Aleppo. On October 16, AFP reported that Syrian troops recaptured the strategic town of Bweida, south of Damascus. According to SOHR, government troops had been supported by Hezbollah and al-Abbas brigade fighters. The next day, the Syrian government's head of Military Intelligence in Deir ez-Zor Governorate, Major General Jameh Jameh, was assassinated by rebels in Deir ez-Zor city. It was thought that he had been shot by a rebel fighter. Then on October 26, Kurdish rebel fighters seized control of the strategic Yarubiya border crossing between Syria and Iraq from Al Nusra after three days of clashes in Al Hasakah Governorate. On November 1, the Syrian army retook control of the key city of Al-Safira and the next day, the Syrian Army and its allies recaptured the village of Aziziyeh on the northern outskirts of Al-Safira. From early to mid-November, Syrian Army forces captured several towns south of Damascus, including Hejeira and Sbeineh. Government forces also recaptured the town of Tel Aran, southeast of Aleppo, and a military base near Aleppo's international airport.

By November 10, the Syrian army had taken full control of Base 80, which is near Aleppo's airport. Then on November 13, government forces captured most of Hejeira, with some pockets of resistance still remaining. The Rebels retreated from Hejeira to Al-Hajar al-Aswad. However, their defences in besieged districts closer to the heart of Damascus were still reportedly solid. For the rest of November the Syrian Army took Tell Hassel, Qara, al-Duwayrinah. At the same time al-Nusra Front and other Islamist rebels captured the al-Omar oil field, Syria's largest oil field.

Rebels led by the Free Syrian army recaptured the historic Christian town of Ma'loula after 3 days of fighting on December 2. In early December, the Islamic Front seized control of Bab al-Hawa border crossing with Turkey, which had been in hands of FSA. The groups also captured warehouses containing equipment delivered by the US In response, the US and Britain halted all non-lethal aid to the FSA, fearing that further supplies could fall in the hands of al-Qaeda militants.

Tension between moderate rebel forces and ISIS had been high since ISIS attacked and captured the border town of Azaz from FSA forces on September 18, 2013. Conflict was renewed over Azaz in early October and in late November ISIS managed to capture the border town of Atme from an FSA brigade. Then on January 3, 2014, the Army of the Mujahideen, the Free Syrian Army and the Islamic Front launched an offensive against ISIS held territory in Aleppo and Idlib provinces.

By January 6, opposition rebels managed to expel ISIS forces from the city of Raqqa, ISIS's largest stronghold and capital of the Raqqa province. On January 8, opposition rebels expelled most ISIS forces from the city of Aleppo, however, ISIS reinforcements from the Deir

Ezzor province managed to retake several neighbourhoods of the city of Raqqa. By mid-January ISIS fighters retook the entire city of Raqqa, while rebels expelled ISIS fighters fully from Aleppo city and the villages west of it.

On January 29, Turkish aircraft near the border fired on an ISIS convoy inside the Aleppo Provence of Syria, killing 11 ISIS fighters and 1 ISIS emir. In late January rebels had assassinated ISIS second in command Haji Bakr, who was al-Qaeda's military council head and a former military officer in Saddam Hussein's army. By mid-February, the Al-Nusra Front joined the battle in support of rebel forces, and expelled ISIS forces from the Deir Ezzor province. By March 2014, ISIS forces fully retreated from the Idlib province. On March 4, ISIS forces retreated from the Aleppo-Turkey border town of Azaz and other nearby villages, choosing instead to consolidate around Raqqa in an anticipation of an escalation of fighting with Al Nusra.

The Syrian army took control of Sahel in the mountainous Qalamoun region on March 4, 2014. Then on March 8, government forces took over Zara, a strategic town in Homs province, further blocking rebel supply routes from Lebanon. Government forces and Hezbollah took control of the Rima Farms region, positioning themselves directly facing Yabrud on March 11. On March 18, Israel used artillery against Syrian Army base, after four of its soldiers had been wounded by a roadside bomb while patrolling Golan Heights.

During March to May 2014 the continued swapping around of captured land continued between the rebels and government forces. On March 23, Hilal Al Assad, NDF leader in Latakia was killed by rebel fighters. The FSA announced on April 26 that they had begun an offensive against ISIS in the Raqqa province, and had seized five towns west of Raqqa city. A truce was put in place on the city of Homs on May 7. The terms of the agreement include safe evacuation of Islamist fighters from the city, which would then fall under government control, in exchange for release of prisoners and safe passage of humanitarian aid for Nubul and Zahraa, two Shiite enclaves besieged by the rebels.

Syria held a presidential election in government-held areas on 3 June 2014. For the first time in the history of Syria more than one person was allowed to stand as a presidential candidate. More than 9,000 polling stations were set up in government-held areas. 11.63 million Syrians were said to have voted. President Bashar al-Assad won the election with 88.7% of the votes.

Starting on June 2, 2014 ISIS forces began to seize swathes of territory in Iraq in addition to seizing heavy weapons and equipment from the Iraqi army, some of which they brought into Syria. Syrian Government airstrikes targeted ISIS bases in Raqqa and Hasakah in coordination with an Iraqi army counteroffensive.

With the extra heavy weapons gained from Iraq ISIS began to capture areas of Syria once more. On July 25, the ISIS took control of Base 17 near Raqqa. Then on August 7, ISIS forces took the 93rd brigade Syrian army military base in Raqqa. ISIS forces took the towns of Akhtarin and Turkmanbareh from rebels in the Northern Province of Aleppo on August 13. The continued cycle of strategic points changing hands continues, as does, rebels and the Syrian Government fighting against ISIS, trying to remove them from Syria. There is no doubt ISIS has changed the course of the Syrian war. It has forced the mainstream

Syrian opposition to fight on two fronts, weakening its stance against Syrian Government forces. It has obstructed aid getting into Syria, and news getting out. By gaining power, ISIS has forced the US government and its European and Arab allies to rethink their strategy of intermittent support to the moderate opposition and rhetoric calling for the ouster of Syrian president Bashar al-Assad.

American and British Special Forces have assisted the rebels and gone in to begin the process of dismantling ISIS. It is a long and slow process and Syria is still very much on the edge - the Assad regiment could still be overthrown, but they finally seem to be slowly regaining control. Special Forces are not in Syria to get involved in the civil war directly. They did aid the training of rebel forces in the initial phase of the Syrian civil war, but the emphasis has been shifted to the elimination of ISIS and preventing them gaining any form of foothold in Syria or Iraq for that matter. As the war continues the Syrian population continue to suffer, sandwiched between a brutal dictatorship and extremist groups.

Chapter Eleven – Islamic State

Syria 1900 hrs August 2014

ISIS has been operating independently of other jihadist groups in Syria such as the al-Nusra Front, the official al-Qaeda affiliate in the country, and has had a tense relationship with other rebels. They have had some military success with the capture of Raqqa in 2014. Baghdadi the leader of ISIS sought to merge with al-Nusra, which rejected the deal, and the two groups have operated separately since. Zawahiri an al-Qaeda chief has urged ISIS to focus on Iraq and leave Syria to al-Nusra, but Baghdadi and his fighters openly defied Zawahiri. Hostility to ISIS has grown steadily in Syria as ISIS regularly attacked fellow rebels and abused civilian supporters of the Syrian opposition. In January 2014, rebels from both Western-backed and Islamist groups launched an offensive against ISIS, seeking to drive its predominantly foreign fighters out of Syria. This inter rebel fight has cost the lives of thousands of rebel fighters.

One such rebel firerfight between Nursa Front and ISIS in mid-2014 when ISIS sent in some fighters to undertake reconnaissance on a village, in preparation for a takeover. The next day 100 ISIS fighters in trucks, some with heavy machine guns and DShKs mounted on them entered the village in order to tempt the Nursa Front fighters out to fight them. In the hope Nursa Front would order in more fighters to reinforce them. Not long after dawn the Nursa Front responded and the snipers started to do their bit taking out ISIS fighters. It was a situation of kill or be killed and what would become an extremely intense firefight in searing Syrian heat.

The initial battle ended the same afternoon it had started when an air strike by a Syrian's Mig-25RB, which destroyed the enemy on the high ground. It had been a hard day of fighting and at times, very intense. The ratio of ISIS to Nursa was about one to one. However the next day 40 ISIS fighters took on nearly 90 Nursa Front fighters, some 3 miles South from Aleppo. In Alepp the ISIS had wanted to push all other rebel fighters out. ISIS had expected to be quite straightforward and only light resistance – however, they soon found themselves under heavy fire just after 8am.

The fire was so heavy, all ISIS could do was crawl and pop up to let a few rounds off, before getting back down low. They could have easily have retreated, but decided to push on instead As ISIS Troop got close to their objective, they split up to take out the Nursa Front PK machine gun positions. The ISIS were trying to get themselves dug in as best as they could under a heavy barrage of enemy fire that had virtually pinned them down. On ISIS fighter in an act of stupidity or bravery. The fighter then charged a machine gun position, which was pinning down 20, ISIS fighters. In the process the ISIS Fighter was shot in the shoulder but continued to charge killing both the Nursa Front fighters manning the machine gun. Once the first machine gun position had been taken out, it turned the tide to their advantage. The ISIS fighters then systematically destroyed every machine gun position in the village, in a very coordinated manner despite running low on ammunition. ISIS had left around eighty odd Nursa Front fighters dead out of an estimated force of around 100. ISIS lost eight fighters in the bloody exchange, further demonstrating their military prowess and ability to attack in a very coordinated manner. This is why, just like the

Taliban, ISIS fighters cannot be underestimated. They fight hard and are well trained. They are not just extremist's with AK47s. One chink in their armour that seems to be growing paranoia, especially in the light of US bombings, which ISIS in many ways thought, would never happen, due to global pressure and America going soft after Afghanistan and Iraq. One example is a group of disillusioned British jihadists who wanted to return home after ISIS were taken prisoner by their commanders. The men were stripped of their weapons and marched to a punishment centre in Raqqa. The five British fighters had complained that they were spending their time fighting other rebel forces instead of the government of Assad and were concerned that they were killing fellow Muslims.

ISIS was thought to have operated an open door policy which has allowed around 250 Britons to return, but the start of US air attacks has made commanders paranoid that spies could direct attacks. All this means, is that the former welcoming atmosphere for Westerners wanting to join the cause has now changed to suspicion as the terrorist group begins to turn on its own fighters.

CHAPTER TWELVE – RUSSIAN LEGACY

It may have been easier to have just sent a team in from Task Force Black and killed Assad not long after the Syrian civil war had erupted, possibly reducing some of the bloodshed. The Russian's did this during Operation Storm 333. Operation Storm 333 was the codename of an operation on December 27, 1979 in which Soviet Special Forces stormed the Tajbeg Palace in Afghanistan and killed Afghan President Hafizullah Amin and his 100–150 personal guards. His 11-year-old son died due to shrapnel wounds. The Soviets installed Babrak Karmal as Amins successor. The operation presaged the Soviet invasion of Afghanistan on the same day. Along with President Hafizullah a further 200 personal guards were also killed.

The operation involved 30 men from the 'Grom' (Thunder) unit of the Alpha Group, 30 men of the 'Vympel' Group and 30 men of the 'Zenit' (Zenith) Group. All three of these forces had been raised by the KGB, for counter terrorism, deep penetration and covert operations. The Alpha Group was more specifically a Special Forces (Spetsnaz) and special operations unit. Attached to the KGB, and had been created on July 28, 1974 within the First Chief Directorate of the KGB on the orders of Yuri Andropov, then chairman of the KGB. It was intended for counterterrorism operations to give the KGB the capacity to respond within the USSR to such incidents as the Palestinian massacre of Israeli athletes at the 1972 Munich Olympics in Germany.

As well as the 90 KGB Special Forces personnel, Operation Storm 333also had 520 men of the 154th Separate Spetsnaz Detachment, made up only of men from the southern republic of the USSR. As well as the 154th, 87 men from the 345th Guards Airborne Regiment. These support troops were not issued with body armour or helmets, whereas the three KGB units had bullet proof body armour and helmets. This was a critical factor as Amin's personal guard totalled around 2,500 men, who were armed only with sub-machine guns, which had low velocity rounds that could not penetrate the Soviet body armour.

The Soviet force approached the target in a convoy of vehicles, many of them in armoured personnel carriers, which were already in Afghanistan as part of the military and technical support for the Afghan government in its fight with major Muslim fundamentalist insurgents in several parts of Afghanistan. By the time of Operation Storm 333, the Soviets had become suspicious of Amin's loyalties and longer term objectives. This made the Soviet come to the decision that he needed to be replaced by a more compliant communist president. As the vehicles approached their large, they were met with ineffective small arms fire and a shower of grenades. A ZSU-3-4 Shilka, normally used for air defence, let rip with its four 23mm cannons with a devastating effect, killing many of the Afghan guards and reducing the shower of grenades along with setting fire to many of the Afghan Vehicles. The Soviets then disembarked from their vehicles and sprinted towards their target. The palace guards continued to fire from the roof with what was now effective fire. The Soviets helmets and body armour protecting the soldiers as they made their way into the target building.

Once inside, each group knew its task and had been fully briefed on the various building internal layouts. Grenades were thrown followed by small arms fire, as each group broke into their assigned rooms and cleared them. As each room was cleared any resistance began to peter out. The Spetznaz finally approached Amin's suite. Amin had been seen earlier, half-dressed shouting to his wife to bring some AK-47s. When the Spetznaz entered the suite, Amin was behind a bar wearing Adidas shorts. As soon as he popped up the first Soviet officer to enter the room and shot him dead.

19 of the Soviet force were killed, along with 50 wounded during Storm 333. Of the 15 dead, two were from Alpha group, three from Zenit group and six from 154th and the rest from the 345th. The Afghan had 200 soldiers killed, 200 wounded and 1,700 captured.

The Russian war in Afghanistan began in February 1979, when the Islamic Revolution ousted the American-backed Shah from Afghanistan's neighbour Iran. The United States Ambassador to Afghanistan, Adolph Dubs, was kidnapped by Setami Milli militants and later killed during an assault carried out by the Afghan police, assisted by Soviet advisers. The death of the U.S. Ambassador led to a major degradation in Afghanistan–United States relations.

The United States then deployed twenty ships to the Persian Gulf and the Arabian Sea including two aircraft carriers. This lead to a constant stream of threats of warfare between the US and Iran. March 1979 marked the signing of the US backed peace agreement between Israel and Egypt. The Soviet leadership saw the agreement as a major advantage for the United States. One Soviet newspaper stated that Egypt and Israel were now "gendarmes of the Pentagon". The Soviets viewed the treaty not only as a peace agreement between their erstwhile allies in Egypt and the U. S. supported Israelis, but also as a military pact. Along with this the U.S. sold more than 5,000 missiles to Saudi Arabia and also supplied the Royalist rebels in the North Yemen Civil War against the Nasserist government. Also, the Soviet Union's previously strong relations with Iraq had recently soured. In June 1978, Iraq began entering into friendlier relations with the Western world and buying French and Italian-made weapons, though the vast majority still came from the Soviet Union, its Warsaw Pact allies, and China. This all set the stage for the Soviet war in Afghanistan, which lasted nine years from December 1979 to February 1989.

It was Part of the wider Cold War, and was fought between Soviet-led Afghan forces against multi-national insurgent groups called the Mujahideen, mostly composed of two alliances – the Peshawar Seven and the Tehran Eight. The Peshawar Seven insurgents received military training in neighbouring Pakistan and China, as well as weapons and billions of dollars from the United States, United Kingdom, Saudi Arabia, and other countries. The Shia groups of the Tehran Eight alliance received support from the Islamic Republic of Iran. Early in the rule of the PDPA government, the Maoist Afghanistan Liberation Organization also played a significant role in opposition, but its major force was defeated by late 1979, prior to the Soviet intervention.

The decade-long war resulted in millions of Afghans fleeing their country, mostly to Pakistan and Iran. Hundreds of thousands of Afghan civilians were killed in addition to the rebels in the war. The initial Soviet deployment of the 40th Army in Afghanistan began on December 24, 1979, under Soviet leader Leonid Brezhnev. The final troop withdrawal started on May 15, 1988, and ended on February 15, 1989, under the last Soviet leader, Mikhail Gorbachev. Due to the interminable nature of the war, the conflict in Afghanistan has sometimes been referred to as the "Soviet Union's Vietnam War" or the "Bear Trap." Over 14,000 Soviet troops, 18,000 Afghan troops were killed along with an estimated 75,000 to 90,000 Mujahideen. It was a war Russia could not win and became an embarrassment to them. However, it set the stage for the Taliban rule of the country until the War in Afghanistan in 2001, when intervention in the ongoing Afghan civil war by NATO and allied forces. The Afghan war followed the terrorist attacks of September 11, 2001, in an effort to dismantle al-Qaeda the prelude to ISIS and eliminate its safe haven in Afghanistan by removing the Taliban from power and putting in place a new government.

However, removing Assad early on would have led to the same power vacuum that has occurred in Iraq and in some ways allowed ISIS to take control. Various rebel forces would have been fighting each other for control of Syria, exactly what has started to happen. If you remove a leader you need to replace it with a strong replacement in the form of a government. But, it is very hard to achieve, as can be seen from both Afghanistan and Iraq.

CHAPTER THIRTEEN – BORDER PATROL

Syrian Border with Iraq 0250 hrs

Barely an hour had passed from our briefing and we were in a Black Hawk racing to our objective, just across the border in Syria from Iraq. The big side doors were slid back and a couple of lads peered into the darkness as the warm Syrian night air hit their faces. We sped fast over the featureless desert, before banking hard and turning to the east. Deko caught the outline of a several palm trees; The Black Hawks were now hugging the ground as we got in close. Trees and vegetation would not only hide us, but also screen out the noise, even though these 'special' Black Hawks were much quieter than normal. Deko made a mental note of the terrain as we got in close, just in case we ended up using it for our escape. Deko liked to plan for every eventually. His idea was that if you planned for the worst, anything that went well was a bonus.

This op had been planned fast like many ops in such a dynamic theatre of war, but you still had to know the choppers had the range to make it there and back, size of force and potential weapons we would be going up against. Intelligence was largely assumptions unless it was feeding real time. You could recce an objective and it had 20 fighters, but by the end of the day when they had all come back from operations it suddenly went to sixty. They could just as quickly change locations and you could get to an objective to find no one there. Using local intelligence who were friendly to us, could prove useful, but again disinformation from locals was not uncommon for one reason or another. Mi5 have been doing their bit, although one of their main focuses is to hunt down Jihadist John along with other Brits fighting or ISIS. The concern is that they will return home to commit acts of terrorism. But ISIS has become a global problem with fighters arriving from countries across the globe. The million dollar question being… What will they do if they decide to return back to their home country?

As soon as we were on the ground we jumped out and quickly made for our objective. It was an old farm in the middle of nowhere, but a high ranking ISIS commander was staying here and we wanted to take him out and gather any intelligence we could. Racing across fields that h decently been ploughed, we could hear voices in some of the nearby farmhouses, and noticed the lights inside flickered.

We were sure that there would be people looking out or on the roof, but through our NVGs (Night Vision Goggles) we could not see any potential snipers. Undertaking an early morning raid helped, as many fighters would be asleep and reduced potential contact, even though once we were in and shooting, the rest of the fighters would soon be woken up by the commotion.

We had an RC-135 circling above keeping a watchful eye and collecting a video feed of the op, that would be used later for our debrief. Having an eye in the sky, meant all exits could be watched and anyone trying to make good their escape could be cutoff or tracked. I looked at my watch and it was 0310 hours, we were on time and were more reliable than dear old British Rail for hitting our objective on time. We needed to get in quick to give the smallest chance possible and the least amount of time to alert ISIS to our presence. We wanted to get our target, as taking out commanders would help towards "cutting the head off a snake." Trudging along, I caught sight of the farm up ahead through the green hues of my NVGs. There was a splash of light from a bulb over the door of what Deko reckoned was our target. Over his headset, the Head Shed had just given him the good news that a Delta Force unit had been informed of our op and would be in position as a cutoff to any ISIS fighters that tried to make good their escape. This gave us one less worry and meant that valuable manpower did not need to be sent round the back of the farm buildings. We could do a simultaneous frontal assault on several farm buildings. The idea was to go in and slot everything we found moving, if we could take the commander alive, we would, but it was highly unlikely he would give us any intelligence unless we could 'pursuade' him that working for us was a better option.

Back at HQ, the Head Shed could see little white shapes walking through the fields towards their forming-up point for the assault barely 100 metres from the small rectangular buildings to be assaulted. The ops room would be full of people pouring over monitors, listening to radio, traffic and communicating to the various resources.

Deko glanced over to see that we were all still there and following him in, before he used hand signals to direct us to our entry points on the farm buildings. We were all dressed in suitable attire, to make us look like rebel fighters. To fool the ISIS into thinking, this was an attack by another rebel force.

We moved onto the first target, and three of us stacked up behind the door, the rest of the team also got into position and Deko and two others formed cover, keeping an eye on windows and doors. One by one we got on the net and said, "in position and waiting for your mark." Finally, after a minute or so that felt like an hour, we go the, "GO, GO, GO."

The lead trooper reached out and carefully tried the door handle. No point blasting your way in if the door was unlocked. Luck was on our side - it was unlocked. Swiftly the lead trooper entered the building, his weapon high, projecting a tight beam of laser light into the black space of the doorway as he went. I could feel sweat trickling down my face, as even though it was the early hours, it was still very warm. There was nobody in there. There could be someone hiding under the floorboards, but we doubted this and moved onto the next building. Head Shed was informed that we had cleared one building as the other teams went in double tapping anything asleep or that moved.

I spotted the nose of a battered saloon car poking around the corner of one building. No idea of the make and model under the grime and faded paint. It was just the car that had been identified as being driven by our main target, so we instantly knew we had the right objective. Just then Deko got on the net, "Be advised all call signs, there's someone on the roof." Scott looked up and quietly said, "Contact!" At almost the same time the muzzle of an Ak47 flashed, sending rounds all around us, I had a great line of sight and opened up my C8, the ISIS fighter on the roof quickly went down, with a clatter on the roof. His fire had been totally ineffective thankfully, not one of us had suffered even a scratch.

With the rest of the ISIS fighters now alerted by the sound of gunfire, we needed to move fast on our main target. I ran with Scott to the main farm building and kicked the door in. There was a second shooter inside. I opened up firing down the main corridor of the farm house, I did not realise until later a single round had hit the body armour I was wearing under my clothes. The house had all its lights on, so my NVGs were rendered useless, so flipped them up and with two others in tow began the room by room clearance. There were several rooms of the main corridor and each one would need to be searched and cleared. With this no longer a silent approach, we may as well lob a stun grenade in each room before going in, if anyone was behind the door, they would open up the minute we poked our head round the door. The first flash bang went off and with the usual flash and crackle. I went in, nothing, "room one cleared," I said over the net. We moved on to room two, Scott through the flash bang in and went in first, he let off several rounds taking out two ISIS fighters who had only just awoken, probably from the sound of my first flash bang. The ISIS fighters AK47s had not yet been picked up let alone make an attempt made to fire them.

As I was assaulting he main farmhouse, another building was also being assaulted, "Two Zero Bravo, room two cleared, one Tango down, moving on to room three." I pushed up the corridor before rounding the door to the last room, with my C8 levelled as I went in. And there, standing in the kitchen, wearing a long, creamy white dish-dash was Tango One, our main target; he was in his mid-forties, with quite a stocky build with a long beard that had twinges of grey in it. He had more hair on his chin than his head. His eyes were filled with hatred - it did not take him long to realise we were not rebels, but western forces and if they read the news reports on the internet would know we were Special Forces. My initial concern was if he was wearing a suicide vest, if so he would blow both himself and me to bits. I had no time to worry, however. As it only took a couple of moments for me to realise he had an automatic pistol in his hand and was about to raise it – I let off two rounds in quick succession straight at the centre of his forehead, he instantly dropped the pistol and dropped to the ground like a large stone. When I went over to check the body and move the pistol away, I noticed that he had been so surprised by us; he had forgotten to remove the safety catch on his pistol. With the final Tango down, I shouted, "Room three clear, building clear."

Deko got on the net to the head shed to inform him that all Tango's had been neutralized and the area was secure. We then started moving through the building methodically, opening all cupboards, tossing the contents of wardrobes, carefully running their fingers along skirting boards and tiling, looking for possible hidey holes. Back and forth we went for a good 20 minutes before someone noticed that in among the jumble of smashed plates on the kitchen floor was a diary.

The rest of the team checked the car outside and all potential nooks and crannies possible looking for potential intelligence or weapons stash, which we would deal with, with some C4. ISIS were careful, although a USB stick was found inside the home of the deceased Abu Abdul Rahman al-Bilawi. The USB stick went on amongst other intelligence to yield the ISIS command structure.

As the team worked their way through they found one ISIS fighter, it did not take long to realise he was a Brit, even though he tried to hide it. He must have hidden himself as we cleared each building, as he did not have as much as a scratch on him. We tried to interrogate him, but he was not saying a word, we forcibly took a DNA sample. We emptied the contents of his pockets, to see if there was anything interesting, all we found was a false ID card, right face but wrong name as we would later find out. Deko tried to interrogate him getting more and angrier with him and his lack of cooperation. I think it was, the fact that, here was a fellow Brit - that would have happily killed one of his fellow countrymen standing in front of him. A red mist of anger and contempt washed over Deko. Looking around the kitchen, his eyes settled quickly on a kind of wooden rolling pin, about a foot long, on the wooden work surface and in one swift move Dekoo swiped it up and smacked the Brit across the face with it. The crack of the impact was followed swiftly by a question, "Who he fuck are you, we will find out anyway, you may as well tell us now." The first blow stunned the British ISIS fighter only momentarily; he mumbled something about Allah and just stared at Deko.

Deko then said "This isn't a fucking social call, mate!" but Brit remained impassive as the scarlet hue of a welt began to appear on his cheek where the staff sergeant had struck him. He was still not prepared to say anything, so it was time to drag the miserable fucker out of the house, gagged and plasticuffed to the rear and led outside before moving towards the awaiting choppers. The Head Shed was pleased with the result, could we have Jihadist John or just one of the many Brits fighting for ISIS.

Deko followed me out into the early dawn sky, and then a couple of trooper's frog-marching their prisoner. Stepping out into the darkness, I flipped my night-vision goggles down again and made my way leading the rest of the assault arty back across the freshly ploughed fields and onto the awaiting Black Hawks for the trip back to HQ just inside Turkey.

We had not caught Jihadist John, but a Brit from Birmingham, who lived not far from where I group up in Bournville, just up the road from the Chocolate factory, where my mum used to work. The Brit would be sent back home and dealt with, depending on if he had been involved in war crimes or terrorism. He would also have to be assessed at what treat he posed to the UK. It was not our job, but the politicians and courts decide his fate, we merely 'tagged and bagged' him for the UK authorities to deal with. Once a British jihadi is in custody, samples will be taken of the suspect's blood and DNA – vital in the case of UK extremists because this information can then be matched to medical records. For identification purposes, a photograph is also taken of the iris – the visible coloured ring around the pupil – which is unique. It is also possible to identify British jihadi on the battlefield by intercepting their radio messages.

CHAPTER FOURTEEN – THE REGIMENT

Growing up in Birmingham, I went to school and later college, with people from a wide variety of different communities. What struck me the most, however, was how in one of my classes, how little the various communities would interact with each other. Preferring to sit in their own group and interact as little as possible with anyone outside of their community. There was a definite tension and I can still remember a Hindu friend giving me a lift home one night - as we passed a Mosque the tirade of racist abuse was something I have never heard before or since.

Racism is often seen as a white problem; however, I have seen more comments made between ethnic minorities than comments from whites. In Syria and Iraq you have Muslim fighting Muslim, countrymen killing countrymen for following the perceived wrong religion or sect. That is one thing about the regiment – yes, we take the piss out of each other and plenty of banter. But the Regiment is a brotherhood and you develop a strong bond with your troop and Regiment. That is something that those that leave, miss, I cannot think of any other job where there is the same camaraderie. We are brothers in arms and no matter what our background or religion share a common goal and work towards that common goal as one. Watching each other's backs, then those who lead us, chastise and praise us like a surrogate mum and dad. The same goes when we work with Delta or the SEALs, these guys are every bit as good as us – although we would never admit it. They are part of our extended family if you like and we watch each other's backs regardless of country or unit.

For the Regiment, it all started the day I turned up for selection...
"Good morning, gentlemen, welcome to Sterling Lines." It was late
winter 2010, a dozen rows of hopeful recruits sat facing the Head Shed,
145 of us in all. The Head Shed gave us all a knowing smile. He knew
of the tough times ahead for us all and that most of us in the room
would not make it through selection. He stood in front of us on the
stage of the training-wing theatre, a slightly weather-beaten figure
dressed in sharply pressed combats and old looking boots. The famous
beret was a little faded, but at the rank of Colonel, he could pretty
much do what he liked. He leaned on the lectern, eyeballing us one by
one, trying to figure out who looked like the ones that would make it
through. He looked like a man in total control, a man who could read
your mind at fifty feet. All of a sudden this voice with a strong
Yorkshire accent said, "You have a difficult task ahead of you. First,
fitness and navigation, four weeks of rigorous selection, during which
time we subject you to what we colloquially and, I might add, very
appropriately refer to as Sickener 1 and Sickener 2. Then, fourteen
weeks of continuation training, jungle training, Survive, Evade, Resist,
Extract. Nearly twenty-eight weeks of exhaustive scrutiny. Half a year
of uncertainty. You could get your marching orders at any point along
the way – usually when you least expect it. We've even been known to
fail someone on their very last day." A look of shock spread amongst
the faces in the room. "If you think passing is easy and you are well
prepared, you are in for a shock. Selection will test you mentally and
physically more than anything you have ever experienced. We only take
the best of the best. Many of you sitting here will fail. The SAS is as

only as good as the men we recruit, we have high expectations and high standards to remain known as the ELITE, revered the world over."

It was not long before we were outside in the grey mist awaiting the first part of selection. As the weeks passed the numbers steadily dropped, until a mere handful of us were left. The Head Shed had been right; this had been by far the toughest test I am ever likely to go through. Here I was lined up waiting to be given the coveted beige beret complete with dagger insignia. I had made it, but was under no illusion of the steep learning curve ahead of me.

Four years on, I have learnt so much and I am still learning. A Squadron mobility troop has been a good place to be. I have had one tour in Afghanistan and there are many similarities with Syria and Iraq. Such as the Taliban using the same 'Insurgents Emporium' for their clothes and equipment as ISIS (this is a joke by the way!). Black is the new green and without an AK-47 in your hand, you're a nobody… Joking aside, the ISIS though, are much more vicious than the Taliban, they seem to enjoy killing more and more focused in battle. Although, the Taliban were a bunch of loons, some high on opium. Once the ISIS threat is diminished, I am sure another bunch of maniacs will replace them in due course.

***

I glanced at my watch. Twenty minutes to go. We sat around in small groups, listening to the ISIS and watching the shadows lengthen as dusk turned to night. We spoke in a whisper and grabbed a quick doze. A couple of the lads ate and washed it down with a brew. If not on stag sleeping or eating was the only form of entertainment, whilst waiting to start an op. You could always get a 4 x 4 out and give your weapon a quick pull through. With little else to do but wait for 'H Hour,' as you wait, the adrenaline does begin to build up especially if it is a more dynamic op.

I stared into the gloom as the great blackness of a moonless night enveloped us. The minutes slipped by as we waited for complete darkness. The rest of the lads checked their equipment and made sure they were all ready to go, like any professional soldier would. Suddenly there was a noise from where the ISIS were. The sound of equipment being moved, the clink of link ammunition being loaded, a rifle falling to the ground, along with the low hum of conversation.

At long last, it was time for us to move off and into the dark night. The troop had gone through the plan that afternoon, so every trooper knew exactly what he had to do. We slowly got up, laden down with equipment and ammunition and made our way forward as soon as the radios clicked to indicate 'h hour.' I began carefully picking my way through the darkness. We led off in single file; I could feel the soft sand beneath my feet. It was hard going and I was soon soaking wet from sweat, we carried on with a slow move forward for just under an hour, drinking regularly to replace lost fluids from sweat. The night was hot and humid, and it started to make you feel weary. Thankfully, it was not that much further even if it was hard going and continued forward before we got into our various FUPs, before commencing the attack. Although as we moved up towards a small group of buildings at the bottom of a valley, which was our objective, the ISIS fighters spotted us and started firing off rounds with little success. We got the GPMG and mortars set up and started to brass down the position, allowing the rest of the troop to advance to our target.

116

As we got close the fire form the ISIS began to get more effective. There was no choice but to 'pepper pot' onto the objective. This movement consists of a soldier getting up and moving forward whilst another is in the prone position giving covering fire, before the soldier moving forward goes firm. The soldier giving covering fire, then gets up and moves past the soldier who has just gone firm and so on. In this case we moved up as a team of four, with two giving covering fire whist two pushed forward.

The fire coming from ISIS was getting quite intense, although still not that accurate. ISIS as usual seemed to be enjoying the fight and put up a fierce barrage over a wide area. They would have been better to have concentrated their fire. The fire support continued to rain down and snipers from six troop were now in position, armed with L82A1 Barret rifles, and took pot shots at various ISIS fighters. The snipers accounted for many of the ISIS fighters killed. While all this was going on, F18 Hornets were on station and began to bomb the main buildings. Our job was to then cut off any fleeing fighters. A couple of F16s, after dropping bombs strafed various enemy positions that were pinning us down, narrowly missing us on one strafing run, which could have led to a blue-on-blue incident.

We made slow but sure progress as every inch was a hard-fought one, such was the strength of the response from the ISIS fighters. We had to conserve ammunition and only fire at targets we stood a chance of hitting, the fire support at our rear would help to keep the ISIS fighters heads down, only popping up to take a shot and reveal themselves to our sniper's. As we got closer to the objective, we did take a casualty, with a shrapnel wound to one of the lad's legs. Rounds were dancing around our feet and ricocheting off the rocks around us. We pushed forward and finally made it to the main buildings and made our way through, clearing buildings and checking for any useful intelligence. The battle had raged for four hours and the base was now littered with ISIS corpses. I vividly remember stepping on something squishy beneath my feet and it turned out to be human entrails that had been ripped out after the poor bugger was blown up and his body scattered over a wide area.

It was a successful op all round, only one casualty and some good intelligence, along with a few more ISIS fighters killed. Reinforcements would be sent. However, we were still in hostile territory, so a tactical withdrawal would be required, to escape undetected by the ISIS or any other rebel forces we tripped over by accident. We returned to our LZ were our transport awaited to take us home, well as close to home as you could get being being just over 2,500 miles from the UK, in a hostile environment.

It is all part of the job - we are here using an array of equipment along with Special Reconnaissance Regiment (SRR) to track down the now infamous 'Jihadist John' down – and hopefully free other hostages being held. Along with reconnaissance and lazering targets for the jets.

Chapter Fifteen – Bug Out

20km North of Raqqa, Syria 2200 hrs

Our mission was to confirm the existence of an ISIS base on the Syrian, Turkey border. A wide open stretch of rugged stretch border, where an estimated seven Britons a week were crossing over to Syria and Iraq. This stretch is simply known as the 'Gateway to Jihad'. One crossing point is on a dry, dusty track that is one of the ancient smuggling routes crisscrossing over the hills to Syria, the border is marked by nothing more than the odd scraps of barbed wire. The path leads down to the Orontes River, which meanders through the valley of olive plantations, and on the other side is Syria. This is an alarmingly easy route to enter Syria. It is where border guards can turn a blind eye for as little as 10 US dollars. An estimated 20 foreign recruits were travelling through it each day on this poorly policed border area, of mountain passes and plains without confronting security. Once in eastern Turkey, British fighters hook up with ISIS handlers and embark on spending sprees in local army equipment shops. They buy hunting knives, sniper rifle sights, binoculars and desert camouflage fatigues. One ISIS fighter, walked into a shop waving $50,000 in bundles of cash as he bought a thousand 'magazine vests' for carrying spare AK47 rifle ammunition clips. For months, Turkey has been reluctant to stop anyone from crossing. They have allowed weapons and supplies destined for recognised Syrian opposition groups to cross and European governments have been frustrated that little appears to have been done to stop the movement of people and weapons.

Under cloudy skies, we dismounted our transport and realised we were going have to detour around an Al Nusra position, the last thing we wanted was to get drawn into any form of confrontation with another rebel force. Syria was more politically charged than Iraq in many ways, in Iraq, we did have support of the government. Although I am sure Assad would be more than happy to see us slot few more rebels. This now meant a longer journey adding a few more hours to our mission. After we had completed our diversion, we were now two hours behind schedule and the longer we were 'out and about' the greater the chance of being caught.

We followed a route that skirted a small village that led to a road. I did sadly miscalculate the distance to the road, losing an hour of valuable time. Deko decided to continue and reach the LUP (Lying Up Position) in a rocky area two hours prior to dawn. Intelligence and aerial photographs showed an uninhabited area, but in fact it was surrounded by Syrian Army forces on one side and an opposing ISIS force on the other. We reached our LUP as day broke. This proved to be far from ideal as a hiding place, as it was surrounded by featureless desert, that was hard to hide in or make much use of dead ground. We hid as best we could between the rocks and spread into a defensive perimeter, one man on stag several metres to the west with a view of the route we had just taken.

As dawn broke, the features of an ISIS position became clear, just under 1km from the LUP. A few hours later, a small ISIS patrol could be seen following the tracks we had left the night before. The ISIS team watched our location for a short while. They then disappeared and then came back with a much larger patrol which passed our FUP.

At around 1800 a four man patrol followed our trail directly to the rocks where we were hiding.

They stopped short of us, and returned to their base. Meanwhile a second ISIS patrol approached the LUP from the other direction, and opened up with heavy fire on our position. As RPGs struck our position, Deko ordered our withdrawal. We had no choice but to double back on the trail that had brought us to our LUP the previous night. We got out with a few scratches not from bullets but from jagged edges on the rocks scrapping our hands as we crawled out. Then an ISIS patrol opened up with an RPD light machine gun, developed in the Soviet Union in 1945 by Vasily Degtyaryov for the intermediate 7.62x39mm M43 cartridge. AK47s also started to rain down fire – luckily for now no more RPGs. We made the assumption that we must have been seen moving up to the LUP. Obviously confused and unsure of our position, they had tried to see if we had moved off or were still there.

Deko and King and made their way in the opposite direction to the rest of us. The small team drew fire as over 20 ISIS fighters began to move up, towards our original position. Bullets were cracking through the air, some ricocheting off the rocks in a series of small sparks. Deko and King started to get some serious fire down, knowing they were both outnumbered and outgunned. Deko knew he could not continue to stay in his current position and would need to move. The fighting continued for about 15 minutes before Deko and King started to run out of ammunition, they had given us a head start and we could loop round and find any available cover to cover Deko and King's exit from the rocks. It was not long before King's and Deko came into view with the odd bullet nipping at their heels, the fire still seemed highly inaccurate, as if they thought a far larger force was present. We had made a lucky escape and gathered very little intel other than coordinates for another ISIS position in Syria, that we could not currently bomb. ISIS must have had a force of around 100 at the base, but thankfully only sent a few out our way. A much larger force, equipped with heavier weapons could have meant a very different outcome. You try not to dwell on the "what if's" just feel happy to have got away and a bit peeved that you were not able to complete the mission. It is all part of the job, and being in the Regiment, taking success and failure in equal measure at times. Very few ops go exactly, according to plan, there are far too many variable to be factored in. The more complex the op, the greater the chance of a Foxtrot Uniform to occur! With Deko and King out of the hot spot and safe, we then carefully made our way back; near to the Turkey border and our ERV (Emergency Rendevous). Where we were eventually picked up by good old Delta Force and taken back to base for a debrief.

The Turkey border has become more intense recently with Kurdish fighters defending Kobane on the Turkey/Syrian border from an advance by Islamic State militants. Kobane has become a flashpoint with an estimated 140,000 civilians fleeing the town and surrounding area over the period of one week. This has then intensified the, with Turkish troops trying to prevent Turkish and Syrian Kurds crossing the border to help defend Kobane from ISIS in the fight of their lives.

It is hard for many people outside of Syria and Iraq to realise the size and scale of ISIS, and that the odd airstrike and Special Forces attacks are not going to get rid of them. A much more sustained attack on a multinational scale is required to cover the vast area the ISIS occupies. Notwithstanding the heavy and hi-tech weapons they possess. As I said earlier in the book, the war against ISIS, will last years, any thought of a quick and decisive campaign has soon been dispelled in Iraq and Syria. ISIS are currently too rich, well equipped and large in terms of numbers of members, which will swell further before any contraction is seen. ISIS have not fully played their hand yet, and will adapt their tactics accordingly. They have a very tactical aware command structure - in the wake of more sustained bombing from the end of Septemeber 2014, ISIS have changed tactics in the face of U.S.-led air strikes in Iraq by ditching conspicuous convoys. 'They don't move in military convoys like they did before. Instead, they are small convoys of motorcycles, bicycles, and if necessary, they use camouflaged cars. ISIS has also taken to placing their flag on the rooftops of residential houses and buildings, many of them empty, to create confusion as to which buildings they occupy. Training to confuse drones and satellites to think these are legitimate targets in which to send bombing missions on. They have also cut back on their use of cell phones as airstrikes have intensified. Another tactic ISIS have used is to take all their furniture, vehicles and weapons. Then plant roadside bombs, before destroying their headquarters. With the more sustained bombing it has led ISIS to go underground in their main Syrian stronghold since Obama authorised U.S. air strikes on the group in Syria. They have disappeared from the streets, redeployed weapons and fighters, and cut down their media exposure, residents said. However, this does not mean air strikes have by no means crippled them. It has meant they will look into hit and run tactics and also start to make greater use of IEDs and use human shields.

Tornado and Typhoon jets from the RAF will add to the arsenal of F-15, F16, F18, AV-8B jets, further ramping up the bombing campaign. The two fronts being worked on, is to cut off the ability to use oil installations and other facilities in territory controlled by the ISIS and quell recruitment, especially from Western countries. The ultimate aim is to roll back and ultimately crush the extremist group that has created a caliphate spanning the Syria-Iraq border.

CHAPTER SIXTEEN – ARAB SPRING

Against the backdrop of Syria and Iraq has been what is called the "Arab Spring" that is part of the wider current unrest in the 'Arab world.' The Arab Spring is a revolutionary wave of demonstrations and protests, riots, and civil wars in the Arab world that began on 18 December 2010 and spread throughout the countries of the Arab League and surroundings. While the wave of initial revolutions and protests had expired by mid-2012, some refer to the ongoing large-scale conflicts in the Middle East and North Africa as a continuation of the Arab Spring, while others refer to the second wave of revolutions and civil wars post 2012 as the Arab Winter. By December 2013, rulers had been forced from power in Tunisia, Egypt (twice), Libya, and Yemen; civil uprisings had erupted in Bahrain and Syria; major protests had broken out in Algeria, Iraq, Jordan, Kuwait, Morocco, Israel and Sudan; and minor protests had occurred in Mauritania, Oman, Saudi Arabia, Djibouti, Western Sahara, and Palestine.

The term "Arab Spring" was used by Western media in early 2011, when the successful uprising in Tunisia against former leader Zine El Abidine Ben Ali emboldened similar anti-government protests in most Arab countries. The term was a reference to the turmoil in Eastern Europe in 1989, when seemingly impregnable Communist regimes began falling down under pressure from mass popular protests in a domino effect. In a short period of time, most countries in the former Communist bloc adopted democratic political systems with a market economy. The events in the Middle East went in a less straightforward direction. Egypt, Tunisia and Yemen entered an uncertain transition period, Syria and Libya were drawn into a civil conflict, Iraq is still unstable and having ISIS begin to take control of parts of the country. While the wealthy monarchies in the Persian Gulf remained largely unshaken by the events.

The protest movement of 2011 was at its core an expression of deep-seated resentment at the ageing Arab dictatorships (some glossed over with rigged elections), anger at the brutality of the government towards the local populous and security regimes in place, unemployment, rising prices, and corruption that followed the privatisation of state assets in some countries. But unlike the Communist Eastern Europe in 1989, there was no consensus on the political and economic model that existing systems should be replaced with. Protesters in monarchies like Jordan and Morocco wanted to reform the system under the current rulers, some calling for an immediate transition to constitutional monarchy, others content with gradual reform. People in republican regimes like Egypt and Tunisia wanted to overthrow the president, but other than free elections, they had little idea on what to do next. With calls for greater social justice, there was no magic wand for the economy. Leftist groups and unions wanted higher wages and a reversal of dodgy privatisation deals; others wanted liberal reforms to make more room for the private sector. Some hardline Islamists were more concerned with enforcing strict religious norms. All political parties promised more jobs, but none came close to developing a program with concrete economic policies. All this was with the backdrop of a world recession and in some cases unrealistic expectations. The expectations that decades of authoritarian regimes could be easily reversed and replaced with stable democratic systems

126

across the region was one failure. It has also disappointed those hoping that the removal of corrupt rulers would translate into an instant improvement in living standards. Chronic instability in countries undergoing political transitions have, put additional strain on struggling local economies, and deep divisions have emerged between the Islamists and secular Arabs. The 2011 uprisings are more a catalyst for long-term change whose final outcome is yet to be seen. Syria, being one example of what the final outcome will be, the same goes for Iraq. One certainty is that ISIS will be driven out, most likely with western intervention, but lessons learnt from the last Iraq war and Afghanistan to ensure a power vacuum is left for the next bunch of maniacs to step up and become the next 'Monster Raving Loony Party.' However, the main legacy of the Arab Spring is in smashing the myth of Arabs' political passivity and the perceived invincibility of arrogant ruling elites. The darker side is the proliferation of extremists forcing their way into a weakened country and trying to grab power. In the Appendix is a more in depth report on the rise of the Jihadist during the Arab Spring.

I do hope you have found this book both entertaining and informative. There is an element of fiction in this book, but mostly it is fact and certainly no bigging up or watering down of what the Special Forces out in Iraq and Syria doing, in a hostile and dangerous war. All the Special Forces are playing a key role and holding back the political hot potato of needing boots on the ground. Working closely with intelligence agencies, Special Forces are doing what they do best, dismantling another terrorist organisation, before the next one appears in a volatile period of Jihadists popping up like mole hills, digging a new network of tunnels in extremism.

There is no doubt that the net is closing in on the allusive Jihadist John and his fellow extremists. With global pressure, ISIS can and will be removed, the element that cannot be predicted is the length of time it will take.

As can be seen, though, the war against ISIS has to be fought on multiple fronts, the SAS and other Special Forces may be the scalpel to get rid of the cancer, but chemotherapy is needed in the form of countries, uniting to prevent extremism within and unite to quell ISIS type uprisings in the first place, before an extremist group has time to take hold and recruit significant numbers into its ranks. Instead, let's breed tolerance and understanding and let it percolate through society at all levels, across the globe.

CHAPTER SEVENTEEN - QUAD BIKE RAIDS

Iraqi Desert near Mosul November 2014

SAS's guerrilla-style raids were introduced in October 2014, targeting main supply routes across western Iraq and vehicle checkpoints set up by the terrorists to conduct kidnappings and extort money from local drivers. These raids have become more and more common, especially in November 2014, with our current raids main intention to degrade Islamic State's fighting capability. Ahead of a spring offensive against ISIS of around 20,000 Iraqi and Kurdish troops early 2015. Various UK forces are providing additional training to the Iraqi and Kurd forces in preparation or the offensive. Although the Kurds would not be able to push further south into Iraq without upsetting the Sunni tribesmen in these areas and the Iraqi army is regarded as a Shia militia. So there will still be barriers to overcome, to fully throw ISIS out of Iraq and I cannot see the SAS, being able to leave any time soon, nor can our commanders if the truth be known.

The whole ethos of our latest raids, though, is to degrade ISIS morale. They have been able to run and hide from some of our planes in the sky, although more often than not miss the drones gathering intelligence on them. It is much harder still, to hide from a sniper in an unknown location or a very fast and fleeting unexpected raid, both SAS specialities. It has taken the level of fear being felt by elements of ISIS to another level. The effectiveness of these raids will be something only time will tell. With an average of eight ISIS fighters being killed a day, the ISIS body count is mounting up and must be ringing alarm bells at ISIS HQ!

Our raids are an echo back to the early raids in WWII and David Stirling. We have replaced the jeep with a Quad bike to perform some daring raids on ISIS positions within Iraq. The change of tactics is to try and disrupt and perform, 'shock and awe' to put the fear of 'God' in ISIS, although I hate to use the term 'God' as there is nothing religious about what ISIS or ourselves are undertaking. However, this short extract from the book "Stirling Work," the story of the Original SAS in WWII, in many ways fits with the use of Quads in the Iraqi desert in both the tactics and potential danger:

"The SAS started to leave Kufta Oasis in Liyia - Mayne was first to leave on 4 September 1942, and then Cumper on 5 September, heading out with their convoy to an RV in the Jebel Mountains. On 6 September, Stirling left Kufta for his 800-mile trek across the desert. Desert navigation is never easy with often very few reference points to go by. The best method was to stick religiously to the bearings, not let doubt creep in and start making adjustments. On 11 September, all three patrols were in the RV. Stirling had heard that an Arab spy had stated that there was now a German Battalion in the North East of the city and some 5000 Italian soldiers scattered around Benghazi. Stirling contacted MEHQ in Cairo and was told by his commanders that it was just 'gossip' and to ignore it.

The convoy of jeeps and lorries left just as the sun was setting on 13 September, although all did not go according to plan. The guide got them lost on the approach to Benghazi, which meant the diversionary raid laid on by the RAF was over before they had made it to the harbour in Benghazi. Driving without lights made it even harder, so Stirling ordered lights to be turned on, instantly making the convoy recognisable to the enemy. At 4:30am, they came to a roadblock with a pillar box just further down the road. The pillar box would need to be taken out before the convoy could progress. Almonds took his jeep down the road, and both sides of the road instantly opened up on the Jeep and the convoy. The Vickers guns on Almonds' Jeep opened up and silenced the Italians for a few seconds. Stirling gave the order to retreat back to the relative safety of the escarpment before dawn. The fast retreat meant the convoy became broken up as the Jeeps and lorries retreated as quickly as they could, knowing that planes may well be sent up to strafe and bomb them. The men made it about 12 miles before they were attacked. Everyone was jumping off the various Jeeps and lorries as the first fighter attacked. Boutinot managed to jump off his Jeep just in time before it exploded under a hail of bullets. Lack of cover was the biggest issue and they knew only luck was going to get them out of this scrape.

They were still 25 miles away from the RV. With the attack over, they had to either cling onto the remaining Jeeps and lorries or walk. They had lost 12 vehicles in total and suffered a few fatalities. Any really badly wounded had to be left where they fell as Stirling, Seekings and Cooper went out to look for stragglers. Over the next couple of days, what was left of the convoy arrived back at the RV. At the RV, a further four seriously wounded had to be left, including a REME fitter who had volunteered to look after the vehicles and saw it as a great learning opportunity. Sadly, all four of the men died in captivity. "

A matter of hours ago we had been preparing for a Quad bike raid. Our Quad bikes were part of a "*£5m contract with UK-based Yamaha and Logic, has provided 200 upgraded all terrain vehicles (ATVs) to ensure quad bikes and trailers continue to provide logistics support on operations.*"

Our Yamaha Grizzly 450 Quads have a top speed of 45mph and are very manoeuvrable especially with the upgraded left hand, dual throttle.

We also have a trailer in which to dump all our heavy weapons and kit, further making them a highly mobile and potent option to perform clandestine raids deep in enemy territory. Weapons can easily be bolted onto them for added 'punch.' In many ways our ATVs are better than the Land Rover 'Pinkies' used in the first Gulf War. They are less observable and a little bit more reliable as well.

Now sitting on the back of my Quad under a dark moonless night, I could hear the distinctive sound of the twin rotor Chinook helicopter fading into the desert. As part of the usual four man team, we had a defined ISIS target to go in and raid and get the hell out. It was around 40 miles to our objective and progress would be dependent on the terrain, although the quads made short work of most surfaces, rocky and steep inclines could reduce speed. The low pressure, chunky tyres made light work of most sandy surfaces, though, almost floating over the sand. We formed up and started our journey following in single file snaking our way through the desert. Initially progress was quite swift. We still needed to be aware of potential ISIS positions or patrols. ISIS over its period of occupation in Iraq has has few fixed operational centres and its chain of command remains mobile. British policy options at this stage are burdened with problems and complications and also bring with them a range of unintended consequences that could draw Western powers into further engagements in the region if we were not careful.

Our targets are picked out from drone intelligence, before hours are spent by intelligence analysts and our chain of command to define suitable targets. Once our senior officers have identified a target, we gather to receive our operational orders. We get an element of input and of course, and spend hours watching video footage ourselves to brief ourselves up and plan the best ingress and egress routes. We can of course deploy our own PD-100 drones as we get close to the target and our preferred method is to stand off and get sniper fire down on the target before bugging out and onto the next target.

The missions have taken place on a near daily basis in the past four weeks and we have expended so much ammunition that our quartermasters have been forced to order a full replenishment of stocks of machine-gun rounds and sniper bullets.

After two hours of driving, we had still not yet reached our target. The final part of the journey involved crossing an Iraqi motorway. The area was a hive of activity, with various Iraqi civilians on them whom could be either friendly or hostile. The problem with crossing the motorway was that the bridge was unsafe due to the high probability of being spotted and the motorway had a large drainage ditch running down the side of it, which the ATV should be able to cross, but we could not be 100% sure. We had no choice but to travel a further few miles on the right hand side of the motorway, looking for a suitable position to cross. We found a junction and left the motorway and made our way across, quickly getting back into the desert and holding short of our target, an ISIS checkpoint, manned by three ISIS fighters. This takedown was going to be by a multiple sniper attack. Deko and King got their Israeli-made DAN.338 sniper rifles out. These rifles are quite a radical design, but can stop a moving car, penetrate armour and kill a man with a headshot from more than a mile away. They are the preferred sniper weapon of the Isralie Special Forces. It also has the highest one shot, one kill ratio of any other sniper rifle and now thought of as the world's best sniper rifle. The SAS began testing them in August 2014 and have quickly been embraced, especially in our current mode of operation. We have and still do use the British-made L115A rifle. But the L115A is heavier, less accurate and has a smaller magazine. It has been in service or 14 years and provided sterling service, but is now outclassed by newer rifles.

King and Deko found a high point that offered a good field of view on the target. They looked down their scope and got two of the fighters lined up in their crosshairs. Before letting off two rounds simultaneously and slotting both fighters with headshots. Deko then lined up quickly and took out the third, who was conveniently sleeping and undisturbed by the soft thud as his to comrades hit the ground dead. The third shot again hit the ISIS fighter in the side of the head - other than slight head and body movement from the impact of the round, impacting on the side of his head entering his brain and more than likely exiting the other side. The ISIS fighter remained in the same slumped position in the driver's seat of the truck looking like he was still sleeping.

With the checkpoint neutralized, we quickly packed up and melted back into the desert before anyone could be alerted to our presence and headed off to our next target. However, this target had moved and there was nothing more for us to do than start heading back; as we did, we noticed a pickup we had spotted earlier had stopped on the motorway and several ISIS fighters had jumped out and were walking around the vehicle, which looked like a Toyota Land Cruiser. We stopped and made sure our guns mounted on our ATV could engage the ISIS fighters if needs be. Due to the position and number it was felt that keeping ourselves hidden was better than taking them on and ISIS reinforcements being called in. Which could lead to a chase through the desert – again something we wanted to avoid. At this point, it did not look like the ISIS fighters had spotted us. The ISIS fighters stayed out of their vehicle for approximately a few minutes before jumping back in and driving away. As dawn drew near we found a good LUP and spent the day there waiting for night fall and moving off on our next series of raids. We spent the next couple of days taking out another checkpoint, sentry post and ISIS commander. Mainly using sniper fire, but did come across a checkpoint and ran through it on our ATVs, hosing it down with machine gun fire, before the ISIS fighters had a chance react. That was our last raid, as we were getting low on supplies and made our way to our extraction point as dawn broke. We called in the Chinook in to extract us and it was not long before the distinctive twin rotor sound of a Chinook was on the horizon once again. In a hail of dust from the Chinook rotors, we drove the ATVs on and flew at low level with the desert flashing by beneath us as we headed back to HQ for a debrief.

The situation in Iraq is very dynamic as it is in Syria and although progress is being made, ISIS still have a firm grip on the region. As of May 2015 they are getting perilously close to Baghdad – if Baghdad falls, will a coalition force of boots on the ground be required again?

If you liked this book then you may like some of Steve Stone's other books:

Delta Force Jericho One – Fast paced story of a Delta oporator on operations in Afghanistan.

Delta Force: Tango Uniform – Follow Delta Force during the 1991 Gulf War searching for SCUDs

Black Ops – special Forces operations from around the world – SAS, Delta, SEALs

Stirling Work - The true story of the original SAS during WWII

GLOSSARY

AK-47 – The AK47 Kalashnikov assault rifle is more commonly known as the AK-47 or just AK (Avtomat Kalashnikova – 47, which translates to the Kalashnikov automatic rifle, model 1947), and its derivatives. It had been and still is with minor modifications, manufactured in dozens of countries, and has been used in hundreds of countries and conflicts since its introduction. The total number of the AK-type rifles made worldwide during the last 60 years is estimated at 90+ million. The AK47 is known for its simplicity of operation, ruggedness and maintenance, and unsurpassed reliability even in the most inhospitable of conditions.

Aérospatiale SA 330 Puma – The Puma was originally manufactured by Sud Aviation of France, and continued to be produced by Aérospatiale. It is a four bladed, twin engine medium lift helicopter. It first flew in April 1965 and is powered by two Turboméca Turmo IVC turboshafts. It has been used in a variety of conflicts and wars around the world and has also proved popular as a civilian transport helicopter.

AV8B – The AV8B was manufactured under licence by McDonnell Douglas and based on the Hawker Sidney Harrier jump jet and later AV8A. Capable of vertical or short takeoff and landing (V/STOL), the aircraft was designed in the late 1970s as an Anglo-American development of the British Hawker Siddeley Harrier. It first flew in 1978 and is powered by a single Rolls-Royce F402-RR-408 (Mk 107) vectored-thrust turbofan. The AV8B is based on the Harrier two, and

produced jointly McDonnell Douglas and British Aerospace. The UK
Harrier fleet was retired from service in 2010.

BTR-80 is an 8x8 wheeled amphibious armoured personnel carrier
(APC) designed in the USSR. Adopted in 1986 and replaced the
previous versions, BTR-60 and BTR-70 in the Soviet Army. It entered
service in 1986 and weighs 15 tons. Powered by a KamAZ-7403 260hp
diesel, it has a top speed of 56mph. Armed with a 14.5 mm KPVT
machine gun and a 7.62 mm PKT machine gun.

Brimstone is an air-launched ground attack missile developed by
MBDA for Britain's Royal Air Force. It was originally intended for
"fire-and-forget" use against mass formations of enemy armour, using a
millimetric wave (mmW) active radar homing seeker to ensure accuracy
even against moving targets. Experience in Afghanistan led to the
addition of laser guidance in the dual-mode Brimstone missile, allowing
a "spotter" to pick out specific targets when friendly forces or civilians
were in the area. The tandem shaped charge warhead is much more
effective against modern tanks than older similar weapons such as the
AGM-65G Maverick, while the small blast area minimises collateral
damage. Three Brimstones are carried on a launcher that occupies a
single weapon station, allowing a single aircraft to carry many missiles.

C8 - The C8 was born out of the C7 when in 1984; Canada adopted a
new 5.56 mm assault rifle. The C7 itself was based on a later version of
the M16. To avoid research and design expenses, the Canadians simply
purchased the license from the USA for a new assault rifle, chambered
for the latest 5.56 x 45 NATO ammunition. This was the Colt model

715, also known as the M16A1E1 rifle. Adopted as the C7, this rifle combined features from both earlier M16A1 rifles and the newest M16A2. Later on, Diemaco (now Colt Canada) developed a short-barrelled carbine version, fitted with telescoped buttstock, which was designated the C8.

Draganov – The Draganov was developed in the Soviet Union as a semi-automatic sniper/designated marksman rifle that fires 7.62×54mm ammunition. The Dragunov has become the standard squad support weapon of several countries, including those of the former Warsaw Pact. The weapon is fed from a curved box magazine with a 10-round capacity, the cartridges are double-stacked in a checker pattern.It has an effective range of 800m and can fire range of low and high powered ammunition.

Eurofighter Typhoon – The Typhoon is a twin-engine, canard-delta wing, multirole fighter. The Typhoon was designed and is manufactured by a consortium of three companies; BAE Systems, Airbus Group and Alenia Aermacchi, who conduct the majority of affairs dealing with the project through a joint holding company, Eurofighter Jagdflugzeug GmbH, which was formed in 1986. It first flew in March 1994 and was introduced into service in August 2003. The Typhoon is a highly agile aircraft, designed to be an effective dogfighter when in combat with other aircraft; later production aircraft have been increasingly well-equipped. Powered by Eurojet EJ200 afterburning turbofan, it has a top speed of Mach 2.

Fairchild Republic A10 Thunderbolt II – The A10 or "Warthog" as it is affectionately known, is a twin engined ground attack aircraft, that carries one of the most powerful guns mounted to an aircraft in the form of the 30 mm GAU-8 Avenger cannon. The A10 first flew on the 10 May 1972 and is powered by two General Electric TF34-GE-100A turbofans also used on the S3 Viking. The A10 has proved itself as a formidable ground attack aircraft in both the Iraq and Afghanistan and able to withstand quite a bit of punishment and still fly.

Dan .338 – The Dan .338, the rifle features a bolt-action. The rifle has been under development since 2010. Chambered in .338 Lapua Magnum, the rifle features a 31" (787.4 mm) heavy-fluted, free-floating barrel with a 1:10" twist. The barrel itself can be quickly changed without specialist tools and features a built-in muzzle break and can be optionally threaded to fit a suppressor. The rifle is fed via a 10-round drop-free box magazine with an ambidextrous magazine release and an ambidextrous safety catch.

DShK – The DShK is a Russian heavy machine gun that came into service in 1938. It is gas operated, with a 12.7x109 mm calibre belt fed and air cooled machine gun. It can be used as an anti-aircraft gun mounted on a pintle. It is also easily mounted to trucks or other vehicles as an infantry heavy support weapon.

General Dynamics F-16 'Fighting Falcon' – The F-16 is a single engine supersonic, multirole fighter aircraft, developed for the USAF. It first flew in January 1974 and is powered by a single F110-GE-100 afterburning turbofan engine. It is one of the most manoeuvrable aircraft in the world and is used by the U.S. Air Force Thunderbirds display team and has been exported to quite a few air forces around the world.

General Atomics MQ-1 Predator – The Predator is a UAV (Unmanned Vehicle) used for reconnaissance of targets and the for battlefield observation. It first flew in July 1994 and powered by a single Rotax 914F turbocharged four-cylinder engine powering a single rear mounted propeller. The MQ-1A has been adapted to carry two AGM-114 Hellfire ATGM or AIM-92 Stinger missiles.

McDonnell Douglas (Now Boeing) F15E 'Strike Eagle' – The F15E Strike Eagle is an all-weather multirole fighter, derived from the McDonnell Douglas (now Boeing) F-15 Eagle. It is powered by two Pratt & Whitney F100-229 afterburning turbofans, 29,000 lbf and capable of Mach 2.5 (2.5 the speed of sound). It first flew in December 1986 and an F15SG version is on order by the ordered by the Republic of Singapore Air Force (RSAF).

Panavia Tornado GR4 - The Panavia Tornado is a family of twin-engine, variable-sweep wing combat aircraft, which was jointly developed and manufactured by Italy, the United Kingdom, and West Germany. There are three primary Tornado variants: the Tornado IDS (interdictor/strike) fighter-bomber, the suppression of enemy air defences Tornado ECR (electronic combat/reconnaissance) and the Tornado ADV (air defence variant) interceptor aircraft. The Tornado

ADV variant is no longer in RAF service having been retired in 2011, being replaced by the Typhoon. Powered by two Turbo-Union RB199-34R Mk 103 afterburning turbofans and a top speed of Mach 2.2. It has proved to be a very successful aircraft and still in front line service. The Tornado was developed and built by Panavia Aircraft GmbH, a tri-national consortium consisting of British Aerospace (previously British Aircraft Corporation), MBB of West Germany, and Aeritalia of Italy. It first flew on 14 August 1974 and was introduced into service in 1979–1980.

Sikorsky UH-60 Black Hawk – The UH-60 Black Hawk has been cemented in history after the books and film 'Black hawk down'. It is a four bladed, twin engine medium lift helicopter designed for the United States Army. It first flew in October 1974 and has been used in a variety of roles and variants since then. Powered by two General Electric T700-GE-701C turboshaft engines, it can carry a variety of payloads and be adapted to suit a wide variety of missions. It was designed from the outset to a high survivability on the battlefield. First being used in combat during the invasion of Grenada in 1983.

Heckler & Koch 417 - The Heckler & Koch HK417 is a rifle manufactured by the German manufacturer Heckler & Koch. It is a gas-operated, selective fire rifle with a rotating bolt and is basically an enlarged HK416 assault rifle. Chambered for the full power 7.62x51mm NATO round, instead of a less powerful intermediate cartridge, the HK417 is intended for use as a designated marksman rifle, and in other roles where the greater penetrative power and range of the 7.62x51mm NATO round are required. It has been adopted for service across the world by armed forces, Special Forces, and police organizations.

Hezbollah – Hezbollah is a Shi'a Islamist militant group and political party based in Lebanon. Hezbollah's paramilitary wing is the Jihad Council; once seen as a resistance movement throughout much of the Arab world, this image upon which the group's legitimacy rested has been severely damaged due to the sectarian nature of the Syrian Civil War in which it has become involved since 2012. Originally founded in 1985, Hezbollah emerged in South Lebanon as a consolidation of Shia militias and standing as a counterpart of the more mature Amal movement. Hezbollah had a significant role in the Lebanese civil war, acting against American forces in 1982–83 and being involved the 1985–88 War of the Camps against Amal and Syria. Ending Israel's occupation of Southern Lebanon, which lasted for 18 years, was the primary focus of Hezbollah's early activities.

Humvee – The HMMWV (High Mobility Multipurpose Wheeled Vehicle), commonly known as the Humvee, is an American four-wheel drive military vehicle produced by AM General. It has largely supplanted the roles formerly served by smaller Jeeps. It has been in service since 1984 and served in all theatres of war. Powered by an 8 Cylinder. Diesel 6.2 L or 6.5 L V8 turbo diesel and with a top speed of over 70 mph, which drops to 55mph when loaded up to its gross weight. It initially lacked any armour, but later version has had some armour protection added against small arms fire.

L115 - The L115 sniper rifle is the British Army adaptation of the Artic Warfare Super Magnum produced by Accuracy International. Designed to achieve a first-round hit at 600 metres and harassing fire out to 1,100 metres, Accuracy International's L96 sniper rifle has also been upgraded with a new x3-x12 x 50 sight and spotting scope. The L115A3 long range rifle fires an 8.59mm bullet which is heavier than the 7.62mm round of the L96 and less likely to be deflected over extremely long ranges.

Lockheed C130 Hercules – The Lockheed C130 Hercules is a four engine turboprop transport aircraft with a high wing design. It first flew in August 1954. Since then there have been many variants used by over 70 countries around the world. Originally powered by four 4 Allison T56-A-15 turboprops. It can carry a payload of around 20,000 kg or up to 92 passengers. It is a highly versatile aircraft and has seen use across the world over its 50 years of continuous service.

M1 Abrahams Tank – The M1 Abrahams main battle tank is a notable tank. One of its more unique features is the fitting of a Honeywell AGT1500C multi-fuel turbine engine. Where most of its contemporaries have used diesel engines. It entered service in 1980, replacing the M60 main battle tank. It has received several upgrades to its weapons systems and armour since introduction. It has a top speed of 42mph on the road and 25mph off road.

M4 Carbine - The M4 carbine is a family of firearms that are originally based on earlier carbine versions of the M16 rifle. The M4 is a shorter and lighter variant of the M16A2 assault rifle, allowing its user to better operate in close quarters combat. It has 80% parts commonality with the M16A2. It is a gas-operated, magazine-fed, selective fire, shoulder-fired weapon with a telescoping stock. Like the rest of the M16 family, it fires the standard .223 calibre, or 5.56mm NATO round.

M16 – The M16 is a lightweight, 5.56 mm, air-cooled, gas-operated, magazine-fed assault rifle, with a rotating bolt, actuated by direct impingement gas operation. The rifle is made of steel, 7075 aluminium alloy, composite plastics and polymer materials. It was developed from the AR-15 and came into service in 1963. The M16 is now the most commonly manufactured 5.56x45 mm rifle in the world. Currently the M16 is in service with more than 80 countries worldwide. It has grown a reputation for ruggedness and reliability and was adopted by the SAS over the less reliable SA80. Later the SAS adopted the C8

.

McDonnell Douglas F4 Phantom – The F4 Phantom is a two-seat, twin-engine, all-weather, long-range supersonic jet interceptor fighter/fighter-bomber originally developed for the United States Navy by McDonnell Aircraft. It first flew on May 27, 1957 and still in service with the Turkish Airforce. The Phantom is a large fighter with a top speed of over Mach 2.2. Powered by two General Electric J79-GE-17A axial compressor turbojets, 11,905 lbf dry thrust (52.9 kN), 17,845 lbf in afterburner (79.4 kN) each. It first saw active service in the Vietnam War.

McDonnell Douglas F/A18 'Hornet' – The F/A18 is a U.S. Navy twin engine supersonic, all-weather carrier-capable multirole fighter jet, designed to be carrier based. It first flew in November 1978 and was initially powered by two General Electric F404-GE-402 turbofans. McDonnell Douglas is now Boeing after being merged in 1997. The Super Hornet is a further evolutionary redesign of the McDonnell Douglas F/A-18 Hornet and first flew in 1995. It is around 20% larger, heavier and has a 41% improved range. As well as avionics, and two General Electric F414-GE-400 turbofans with 35%more thrust than the original Hornet.

Mi-25 also known as the 'Hind D' is a Russian designed and built attack helicopter, gunship and troop carrier. It is a large attack helicopter and heavily armoured, it first flew in 1969 and has seen use, with a variety of armed forces across the globe. Over 2,300 have been built so far. It was developed from the Mil Mi-8 transport helicopter. It is powered by two Isotov TV3-117 turbines, 2,200hp each and a top speed of 208 mph and a range of 280 miles. The Mi-25 weighs over 8 tons empty and is 57 feet long and 21 feet high.

PK - The Kalashnikov PK is a 7.62 mm general-purpose machine gun designed in the Soviet Union. The PK machine gun was introduced in the 1960s and replaced the SGM and RP-46 machine guns in Soviet service. It remains in use as a front-line infantry and vehicle-mounted weapon with Russia's armed forces, and has been exported extensively. It can fire at 650-750 rounds a minute from belts in 100/200/250 round boxes.Fired from the ground from either a Bi-pod or tripod and an effective range of 1,500m.

RC-135 Rivet Joint – The Boeing RC-135 is based C-135 Stratolifter airframe, and is a four engine wept wing intelligence gathering plane, used by the United States Air Force. More recently three have been purchased by three RAF to replace the Nimrod R1 and MR1. The C-135 is essentially a military version of the Boeing 707 and first flew on 17 August 1957. The RC-135 was ordered in 1962 and was a modified version of the C-135A. A total of nine were originally ordered. In total there is currently 32 in operation, including the first delivery to the RAF. The RAF version is the latest RC-135W Joint River, converted from KC-135R airframes first delivered in 1964. Powered by four CFM International F-108-CF-201 turbofan engines, producing 22,000 lbf (96 kN) each. They are the same engines as used on the current Boeing 737 800.

RPD Light Machine Gun is an automatic weapon using a gas-operated long stroke piston system and a locking system recycled from previous Degtyaryov small arms, consisting of a pair of hinged flaps set in recesses on each side of the receiver. It fires 7.62 mm ammunition from a cylindrical metal container that clips on and holds 100 rounds. It can fire 650-750 rounds per minute is an effective ire support weapon. For firing from the prone position, as well as adding stability when firing, a bipod is fitted to the front of the weapon.

The RPG-7 is a portable, unguided, shoulder-launched, anti-tank rocket-propelled grenade launcher. Originally the RPG-7 and its predecessor, the RPG-2, were designed by the Soviet Union. The ruggedness, simplicity, low cost, and effectiveness of the RPG-7 has made it the most widely used anti-armour weapon in the world. Currently around 40 countries use the weapon, and it is manufactured in a number of variants by nine countries. The RPG has been used in almost all conflicts across all continents since the mid-1960s from the Vietnam War to the early 2010s War in Afghanistan.

SR-25 (Stoner Rifle-25) is a semi-automatic special application sniper rifle designed by Eugene Stoner and manufactured by Knight's Armament Company. It fires 7.62mm ammunition and came into service in 1990, first being used in anger in Somalia in 1993.

Sikorsky UH-60 Black Hawk – The UH-60 Black Hawk has been cemented in history after the books and film 'Black hawk down'. It is a four bladed twin engine medium lift helicopter designed for the United States Army. It first flew in October 1974 and has been used in a variety of roles and variants since then. Powered by two General Electric T700-GE-701C turboshaft, engines it can carry a variety of payloads and be adapted to suit a wide variety of missions. It was designed from the outset to a high survivability on the battlefield. First being used in combat during the invasion of Grenada in 1983.

T-62 is a Soviet main battle tank produced between 1961 and 1975. It became a standard tank in the Soviet arsenal, partly replacing the T-55, although that tank continued to be manufactured in the Soviet Union and elsewhere after T-62 production had ceased. The T-62 was later replaced in front-line service by the T-72. Powered by a V-55 12-cylinder, 4-stroke one-chamber 38.88 litre water-cooled diesel engine, developing 581hp. The T-62 has a top speed of 31 mph on the road and 25 mph cross country.

T-72 is a second generation tank entering service in 1973 and went on to become the most common tank used by the Warsaw pact. Its basic design has been used in the T-90. It weighs 41 tons and has a 125 mm 2A46M smoothbore gun, 7.62 mm PKT coax machine gun and 12.7 mm NSVT antiaircraft machine gun. Powered by a V-12 diesel, with 780 hp and a top speed of 37 mph. Over 25,000 have been produced so far and it currently remains in production.

Toyota Hilux – The Toyota Hilux is a small pickup truck manufacture by Toyota in Japan. It has been produced since 1968 and is currently on its 7th generation. It can have either front wheel drive or four wheel drive. The Hilux has gained a reputation for exceptional sturdiness and reliability, even during sustained heavy use and/or abuse, and is often referred to as "The Indestructible Truck".

Yamah 450 Grizzly - The Yamaha Grizzly is a large utility all-terrain vehicle manufactured by the Yamaha Motor Company. Introduced in 2003 as a 2004 model, it was a huge leap forward relative to its competition. It uses many light-weight materials to give it the lowest dry-weight (350 lbs.) of any 450-class sport ATV. Powered a Single cylinder 449cc, liquid-cooled, 4-stroke, DOHC, 5-valves.

ZSU-23-2 – The ZU-23-2 "Sergey" is a Soviet towed 23 mm anti-aircraft twin-barrelled autocannon. It was designed to engage low-flying targets at a range of 2.5 km as well as armoured vehicles, at a range of 2 km and for direct defence of troops and strategic locations against air assault usually conducted by helicopters and low-flying airplanes. Normally, once each barrel has fired 100 rounds, it becomes too hot and is therefore replaced with a spare barrel.

Appendix I

Islamic State: Where key countries and Iran

Regional Shia power Iran has seen ISIS - which regards Shia as heretics who should be killed - advance to within 25 miles (40km) of its border.

Although Iran stands on the opposite side of much of the international community over Syria, it has called for co-operation against ISIS. It has reached out to its rival Saudi Arabia - the leading Sunni power - and turned a blind eye to US actions in Iraq, which it has historically opposed.

In Iraq, the Iranians themselves have played a key role in countering ISIS. Revolutionary Guards have advised Iraqi security forces, Iranian pilots have carried out air strikes, and Iranian-backed Shia militia have been mobilised.

Iran says it has also been sending weapons and advisers to Iraqi Kurdistan. In addition, Tehran joined Washington in withdrawing support for Iraqi Prime Minister Nouri Maliki in August.

US Secretary of State John Kerry opposed Iran's attendance at an international conference in Paris in September on helping the new Iraqi government fight ISIS, but stressed that he was still prepared to discuss Iraq and Syria with the Iranians. Iranian officials, meanwhile insisted that they had rejected multiple invitations by the US to join the coalition.

Iraq

The former Shia-dominated government of Nouri Maliki marginalised Iraq's Sunni community, creating conditions which helped the extremist Sunni ISIS come to prominence.

The US hopes Prime Minister Haider al-Abadi's new administration can win the support of Iraq's Sunnis

When ISIS overran the northern city of Mosul in June before moving southwards, Mr Maliki requested US air strikes. However, US President Barack Obama said further military assistance was dependant on an inclusive government being formed.

He nevertheless launched air strikes in August when thousands of members of the Yazidi religious minority became trapped on Mount Sinjar.

In September, Mr Maliki stepped aside and a new Iraqi government was named. The next phase of US assistance will reportedly involve an intensified effort to train, advise and equip the Iraqi military, Kurdish Peshmerga fighters and Sunni tribesmen willing to turn against ISIS.

It is not clear how new Prime Minister Haider al-Abadi will deal with the Shia militiamen who have stopped ISIS reaching Baghdad. Some have been accused of operating outside of the state's control and carrying out reprisal attacks against Sunnis.

At the end of August, Mr Abadi vowed to rebuild the Iraqi army and to create a new "national guard organisation" modelled on the Sunni Sahwa (Awakening) councils that battled al-Qaeda alongside US troops.

Syria

Since the start of the uprising against his rule in March 2011, President Bashar al-Assad has repeatedly warned of the threat of Islamist extremists to Syria and the wider region.

Western powers initially dismissed Mr Assad's portrayal of his opponents as "terrorists", but became increasingly concerned by the rise of ISIS and al-Qaeda's affiliate, al-Nusra Front, in Syria.

The US is relying on "moderate" Syrian rebels to take the fight to ISIS

Top US general Martin Dempsey has warned that ISIS cannot be beaten without attacking its strongholds in Syria. That has prompted questions about whether to co-operate with the Syrian government, which has offered to assist the international community in the fight against ISIS.

However, Washington and its allies still want Mr Assad out of power. In September, Mr Obama announced he had authorised air strikes in Syria, despite concerns over their legality, the threat of Syria's air defence system, and the fact that they might benefit Mr Assad. Instead, Mr Obama is relying on Syrian rebels to take the fight to ISIS and has called on the US Congress to authorise his plan to train and equip "moderate" groups.

Turkey

Turkey is eager to defeat ISIS, which has advanced into territory along its borders with Syria and Iraq. However, it refrained from signing a communique that committed a number of Middle Eastern states to take "appropriate" news measures to counter ISIS, frustrating US officials.

Ankara's response has been reportedly restrained out of concern for the 49 Turkish citizens kidnapped by the jihadist group in Mosul in June.

Turkey has nevertheless offered to allow humanitarian and logistical operations from Nato air bases on its soil. The authorities have also attempted to stem the flow through Turkish territory of jihadists wanting to join ISIS. Turkey has been one of the most vocal critics of President Assad and it became the primary route into Syria for foreigners wanting to fight alongside the rebels. Since the start of the year, more than 450 foreigners have been detained or deported and Turkish security forces have sought to close smuggling routes.

Turkey is anxious that weapons sent by Western countries to Iraqi Kurdish Peshmerga forces do not end up in the hands of the Kurdistan Workers' Party (PKK) - designated a terrorist group by Ankara, the US and EU - which has joined the fight against ISIS in northern Iraq.

Saudi Arabia

Regional Sunni power Saudi Arabia has been a key supporter of Syrian rebel forces, including hardline Islamist groups, but it has rejected an Iranian accusation that it has directly supported ISIS. However, wealthy Saudis have sent donations to the group and some 2,500 Saudi men have travelled to Syria to fight.

Saudi Arabia recently sent thousands of troops to its border with Iraq

The Saudi authorities are concerned that ISIS will inspire Saudi jihadists to challenge the monarchy's legitimacy and seek to overthrow it. King Abdullah has called for "rapid" action.

In July, Riyadh deployed 30,000 troops to beef up security along its border with Iraq, and the following month hosted Iran's deputy foreign minister as the two regional rivals agreed to co-operate.

The Saudi government hosted a meeting in September at which regional states vowed to "do their share" to combat ISIS. Riyadh has

154

agreed to a US request to provide a base to train Syrian rebels, but Foreign Minister Prince al-Waleed bin Talal has said he does not believe his country will participate in military operations.

Jordan

Jordan, a staunch US ally, has security services and a military that could support efforts to combat ISIS. The group has threatened to "break down" Jordan's borders, although it is not thought likely to launch an assault anytime soon.

The Jordanian military has nonetheless doubled its military presence along the border with Iraq. King Abdullah II attended the Nato summit in Wales in September, where the alliance discussed how to deal with ISIS.

Within Jordan itself, ISIS enjoys the support of a growing number of people, some of whom staged demonstrations in the southern town of Maan in June, and more than 2,000 Jordanian citizens are believed to have travelled to Syria to fight. The king has long called on Syria's President Assad to step down and has reportedly allowed Jordan to become a staging ground for the rebels and their foreign backers.

Lebanon

Lebanon has become deeply divided by the conflict in Syria, and has had to deal with an overspill of violence and a huge influx of refugees. In August, Syria-based ISIS fighters raided the border town of Arsal, killing and kidnapping dozens of Lebanese security personnel. Jihadist militants have also carried out a series of deadly bombings in Beirut and elsewhere.

They have mostly targeted Iranian facilities and Hezbollah, the Lebanese Shia Islamist group whose fighters have played a key role in helping turn the tide in President Assad's favour. Lebanese Prime Minister Tammam Salam has warned that the spread of ISIS poses "a big test that our destiny depends on". His country's many religious and political factions have been urged to put aside their differences to ensure the group does not establish a foothold.

United Arab Emirates

The UAE is believed to have offered its air force to attack ISIS positions in Iraq. It is vehemently opposed to Islamist groups in the region, particularly the Muslim Brotherhood, and is believed to have launched air strikes on Islamist-allied militia in Libya from bases in Egypt in August.

Qatar

Qatar has rejected accusations from Iraq's Shia leaders that it has provided financial support to ISIS. However, wealthy individuals in the emirate are believed to have made donations and the government has given money and weapons to hardline Islamist groups in Syria. Since ISIS launched its offensive in northern Iraq in June, the Qatari authorities are reported to have repaired relations with other Gulf states who accused it of meddling in their affairs.

Other Arab states

Egypt, Kuwait, Bahrain, Oman joined Saudi Arabia, the UAE, Qatar, Iraq, Jordan and Lebanon in signing a communique at a meeting in Jeddah that declared their "shared commitment to stand united against the threat posed by all terrorism". They pledged to provide military support and humanitarian aid, and to halt the flow of funds and foreign fighters to ISIS.

Russia

Russia is one of President Assad's most important allies, providing it with diplomatic and military support. It has vetoed several UN Security Council resolutions condemning his deadly crackdown on peaceful dissent and continues to supply the Syrian military with weapons and aircraft.

Moscow's actions have prompted ISIS fighters to vow to oust President Vladimir Putin and "liberate" the North Caucasus. Russian security services believe hundreds of militants from Chechnya and other Caucasus republics have joined ISIS, including prominent commander Omar al-Shishani.

In July, Russia delivered the first batch of 25 Sukhoi fighter jets to Iraq to help boost the firepower of its air force and it attended the Paris conference that discussed how to deal with the threat of ISIS.

European Union

France has signalled that it is prepared to launch air strikes in Iraq and send special forces personnel to the country to help direct them and to train Iraqi government forces. It is already carrying out reconnaissance flights and providing weapons to Kurdish fighters in northern Iraq. Paris has at the same time expressed concerns about air strikes in Syria.

French Kurds protest in Paris against ISIS (16/08/14)

France is one of a number of countries sending arms to Iraqi Kurds to fight ISIS

The UK has said that no decision has been made about how it will be involved in the fight against ISIS, but that it would play a "leading role". It has not ruled out air strikes in Iraq or Syria, but has said targeting ISIS positions in the latter would be complicated. MPs voted against the government's plans for military action in Syria a year ago.

157

Germany has said it has a "humanitarian responsibility... to help those suffering and to stop ISIS". It has provided weapons to Kurdish fighters but ruled out air strikes.

Source:BBC News

APPENDIX II

JIHADI DISCOURSE IN THE WAKE OF THE ARAB SPRING

This report analyzes jihadi discourse in the wake of the "Arab Spring" to address two related questions: (1) why have global jihadi leaders been struggling to advance a coherent and effective response to the events of the Arab Spring, and (2) why, despite strong rhetoric of militancy, have we witnessed little action on the part of new jihadi groups that have emerged in countries that underwent regime change (i.e., Tunisia, Egypt and Libya) as a result of the Arab Spring? To answer these questions, this study focuses on original Arabic sources in the form of public statements released by global jihadi leaders in response to the Arab Spring and by new groups projecting a jihadi worldview that have emerged in Tunisia, Egypt and Libya. It reveals that the factors that are causing the current ideological incoherence of jihadism are the same factors that had once served as the cornerstone of its plausibility in the eyes of its adherents. As to new jihadi groups, this study highlights the inconsistency between their rhetoric and their actions. While they uphold the principle of the obligation of jihad, advance anti-democratic rhetoric using religious arguments and lionize global jihadi leaders and their causes, for now these new jihadi groups are characterized more by the propaganda of jihad than by its delivery. While Syria has not undergone a regime change, but in view of the proliferation of militant groups there, some of which are operating under a jihadi banner, the concluding section of the report nevertheless discusses the implications of the situation in Syria on jihadism. This study argues that the events in Syria could have restored the credibility of jihadism, but competition between the Islamic State of Iraq (and the Levant) and the Syria-based jihadi group Jabhat al-Nusra (JN) has confused and divided their supporters and earned the derision of their opponents. The divide between the two groups, even risks undermining the symbolic position that Ayman al-Zawahiri occupies as the global leader of jihad.

Bibliography

Barry Davis *Heroes Of The SAS: True Stories of The British Army's Elite Special Forces Regiment* (Virgin Books; New Ed edition 2007)

Chris Ryan *The One That Got Away* (Red Fox; Junior Ed edition 2010)

Damien Lewis *Bloody Heros* (Arrow; New Ed edition 2007)

John parker *SBS: The Inside Story of the Special Boat Service* (Headline; 2nd Revised edition edition 2004)

Mark Nicol *Ultimate Risk* (Macmillan 2003)

Mark Urban *Task Force Black* (Abacus 2010)

Micahel Ahser *The Regiment: The Real Story of the SAS* (Penguin 2008)

Peter Scholey *The Joker: 20 Years Inside the SAS* (Andre Deutsch Ltd; New edition edition 2007)

Peter Winner *Soldier 'I': the Story of an SAS Hero: From Mirbat to the Iranian Embassy Siege and Beyond* (Osprey Publishing 2010)

Internet

www.daily-mail.co.uk

www.bbc.co.uk/news

CPSIA information can be obtained
at www.ICGtesting.com
Printed in the USA
LVOW04s0311081215
465794LV00034B/1770/P